The Passage Falcon

By

Bob Dalton

Falcon Leisure Publishing

Falcon Leisure Publishing

First published 2015
ISBN: 978-0-9572213-1-4

Published by: Falcon Leisure Publishing,
Pointers Rest, 1 Witt Road, Fair Oak,
Eastleigh, Hampshire, SO50 7FW.

Editing: Bob Dalton
Proof Reading: Diana Durman-Walters
Layout and design: Lorraine Proctor

Produced by: Solent Design Studio Ltd,
Claylands Road, Bishop's Waltham,
Hampshire, SO32 1BH.

DEDICATION

This book is very respectfully dedicated to those that have had a profound effect on my thinking and subsequent actions when it comes to training and flying any hawk or falcon. Through either their writings, or direct conversation in some cases, they have shaped my ethical as well as moral code of conduct when it comes to falconry and to a certain extent life itself. By dedicating this book to them and their memory I in no way purport to being anywhere near the same calibre of falconer as them. However I would like to think that is how I have lived my life as a falconer and as a man would not have displeased them or given them cause to disown me.

Accordingly I dedicate this book to Simon Latham, Gilbert Blaine, Geoffrey Pollard, Ronald Stevens, Michael Woodford, Stephen Frank, Roger Upton and Lorant De Bastyai. Last, but by no means least, there will always be a deep respect and fondness within me for Ceri "Griff" Griffiths, a man happy to share what he had with those who would appreciate what he was sharing.

I would also like to acknowledge the deep gratitude I have towards Diana Durman-Walters for the encouragement to write this book and the hours she spent proofreading it and then convincing me she was right and I was wrong when it came to changes.

FOREWORD

The Passage peregrine is a recollection of falconry experiences past and present by Bob Dalton. The art of flying a passager is an acquaintance that very few falconers in the UK will have had the pleasure of, yet during the course of falconry history this would have been accessible to those that chose to fly peregrines. Accomplished and well-practiced falcons in the wild, they bring their skills to the falconer, creating quite remarkable hawking.

Despite the fact that the few elements of contact in the UK will only be with falcons that require rehabilitation, there are many other countries that allow a level-headed harvest of passage peregrines, and these are principal to those falconers and their sport.

Bob Dalton's falconry experiences, spanning close on 50 years, has been a love affair with falcons, but especially the passage peregrine, whose ability and accomplishments have singled her out as the perfect hawking companion, when seeking flights that are of the highest calibre. Having been fortunate to fly them himself as well as be in the company of falconers that fly no other type of falcon, the Passage Peregrine is a tribute to all that is dazzling in this style of falconry. The book conveys the essence of these peregrines through the superb art work of Carl Bass, which visually enhances Bob Dalton's knowledgeable and vivid writing.

Diana Durman-Walters
June 2015
Cornwall

CONTENTS

INTRODUCTION

"Man has emerged from the shadows of antiquity with a Peregrine on his wrist. Its dispassionate brown eyes, more than any other bird, have been witness to the struggle for civilization, from the squalid tents on the steppes of Asia thousands of years ago, to the marble halls to European Kings in the seventeenth century." (Roger Tory Peterson)

When I first set out to write this book a great many of my falconry orientated acquaintances expressed the opinion that I was wasting my time and that this was a book that was quite simply beyond its time and had no real relevance. Accordingly it would serve no useful purpose other than to look back on things as they were a great many years ago and therefore any energy expended on writing it would be better and more profitably spent directed elsewhere. The general consensus seemed to be that for probably the vast majority of falconers it would look back to times they never ever had any first hand experience of and for that reason, so I was repeatedly told, it could not possibly be of interest or commercial value. All of this somewhat negative advice was given; I am sure, with regard and well meant intention and not as a form of criticism or mild derision.

The fact that I have doggedly set out to write this book shows that I disagreed with the discouraging statements sufficiently to continue with the work anyway. Not that I disagreed with all the sentiments expressed particularly as to such a book not being a likely commercial success. Surely for a falconer money is not the motivation for putting down thoughts and experiences gained over a lifetime of practising and following avidly the sport that is dearest to their heart. I believe it is more a case of gaining pleasure from sharing the experiences that have brought joy and enrichment to the life of the author. It's like listening to a beautiful piece of music or watching a wildlife spectacle, it means so much more when you can share the moment with someone who also appreciates such things.

The doubts raised that those who were too young to have known the joy of flying passage falcons would not be interested in the subject I have to say I both agree and disagree with to some extent. I know that sounds like I am sitting on the fence but I will explain my reasoning. There is a generation of falconers in the twenty-first century that seem to have many different values to those falconers of my generation. Not all by any means, but probably the majority, I speak here primarily of those to be found in Great Britain. A whole generation has grown up were quantity instead of quality, with regards to kills in the field, seems to be the bench mark of success and old traditional means of training and hawk husbandry have, to a degree, fallen by the wayside. The use of tirings and rangle, or even knowing what they are, being two very obvious examples. The very language of falconry, so rich and admirably suited to describing hawks, their needs and their habits, is very fast disappearing. You speak to a modern falconer now and tell him you are flying a falcon that was disclosed three seasons ago and he will look at you as if you are talking an alien language or have escaped from some home for the mentally impaired. The proliferation of the domestically produced Harris Hawk and its ready availability to new comers to the sport have spawned a new hawking culture that, in many cases, leaves me wondering about the general future and well being of falconry and hawking.

On the other hand there are those that are passionate about their falconry and want to understand as much as possible about it as well as thoroughly immerse themselves in it and its past. These falconers will take an almost scholarly interest in falconry not only as it is now but also as it was in the time before they personally practised it. For these falconers this book will hopefully prove to be of interest and if nothing else will let them experience the joy of the passage falcon through someone else's eyes and someone else's thoughts.

When it comes to whether or not I should expend the effort in writing a book like this then probably one of the main questions would be "Is there still a place for the passage falcon in modern falconry". With the advent of domestic production of hawks, the proliferation of hybrids artificially giving the falconer ever bigger and more powerful falcons should he want them, the use of both tame and wild hack to improve initial fitness and dexterity, it would be all too easy to dismiss both the desire and need by the modern falconer for the passage falcon. For those that think why train a wild taken hawk with all the difficulties that usually accompany such an undertaking, when I can have a bigger, better behaved domestically produced hacked falcon, without the heart stopping moments associated with the wild falcon, then this book is definitely not for you. For the falconer that glows with an inner pride when his passage falcon allows him to take her up from a kill without any fuss or bother and waits for him to help her break in, or returns to the lure after an unsuccessful flight and waits patiently to be taken back up onto the fist, no matter how many seasons he has been flying her, then this book is one I want to share with you.

The passage falcon, in my mind, will undoubtedly always have its place in falconry and that place is surely on somewhat of a pinnacle. No disrespect intended to any other form of falcon, no matter what the species, but the passage hawk will always be superior in the hands of a falconer who knows how to guide his falcon through her training and hunting. I say guide, because I personally don't believe we train falcons rather we encourage them to work in co-operation with us and trust that they get to realise that working with us is a worthwhile exercise for them. In traditional falconry the passager was, for a number of centuries, considered only suitable for flights out of the hood. These were mainly at Heron and Kite in Europe, Cranes in Japan and Kite and Grass Owls in India. At this time, the sixteenth and seventeenth centuries, there was no falconry in what has now become the United States of America and Canada. In fact much of this huge tract of land was unpopulated till considerably later, although it has to be said falconry in a few short decades galloped ahead in these countries and more than caught up with their European and Oriental counterparts.

In many of the countries throughout the world, where falconry is still practised, the taking of passage falcons is now either illegal or severely restricted. It has to be said that this, in the vast majority of cases, is undoubtedly a good thing. The health of the wild population must always take precedent over the sporting desires of individual falconers. However there are some countries where the taking of passage falcons for use in falconry is still not only legal but also completely ethical. One or two countries have no laws relating to taking falcons from the wild, others have a licensing system that severely restricts the numbers taken and this system itself is dependent on wild population dynamics. The vast majority of true falconers are more than happy to go along with such licensing systems as they would never want to do anything that would have repercussions of a negative nature on the wild populations.

The United States of America for instance has instigated a quota system for the taking of a limited number of passage falcons each year and this is done by a state by state basis with a very small take being allowed in each relevant state. At the time of writing the total number of the take for the entire country is just one hundred falcons. However it is still one hundred more falcons than were allowed to be taken a few years ago. Added to this with each year that passes more and more falconers will be getting their passage falcons as the same people won't be applying over and over again. Some will obviously lose their falcons at some stage and then re-apply, but the majority of falconers will get their passage falcon and be perfectly content with their lot for a considerable number of years. This particular system is far from foolproof, but then of course what system is ever going to truly be so. However it is a basically fair system and seems to satisfy the criteria set down by the conservationists and falconers alike. The falcon in question that American falconers are allowed to take at the moment is the Arctic Tundra Peregrine Falcon (falco peregrinus tundrius) and is taken as it migrates down from the North heading for the sunnier climes of South America in general and Patagonia in particular.

Passage Falcon

With this is mind I revert to my original question regarding the writing of this book and the place of the passage falcon in modern falconry. Obviously my opinion is somewhat biased, as I am determinedly setting out to write the book, and I hasten to add that as I do so, am fortunate enough to look out my office window and watch my passage falcon "Gillian" preening herself in the afternoon sun that we are fortunate enough to be enjoying on this particular day. On the next perch is "Gale" an intermewed falcon gentle who, due to a foot injury, seems destined to stay with me on a long term basis. Up until three seasons ago I had been flying a passage tiercel and we had enjoyed the best part of eleven seasons of extremely mixed fortune together. These falcons I mention here, along with a great many others, have all come to me, through various channels, to see if they can be rehabilitated back to the wild following some mishap or another. The majority can be restored to full health and fitness and eventually put back into the wild where they belong. A few are destined not to be able to return to the wild but are still capable of being flown for falconry.

A good example is the passage tiercel mentioned. He suffered a broken wing and was left by a so called knowledgeable rehabilitator in an aviary so that the wing could heal itself. In due course the wing bone did knit but not in true alignment. The tiercel was able to be trained in the conventional sense of the word and eventually hunt again but only by flying him every other day. The day after flying he wouldn't hold his wing in the correct position so in the wild would obviously struggle. From a falconry point of view however it meant I could fly him every other day and give him full crops on the days he did fly followed by reduced rations the following day. This regime worked well for both of us and this tiercel took both grouse and partridge. Other falconers throughout the world are undoubtedly enjoying the delights of flying passage falcons and with the general increase throughout the world in the population of the Peregrine Falcon, in all its glorious forms, I for one can only see things, from a falconer's perspective, improving long term.

In this book I have absolutely no intention of going through the long, tedious and mind numbing process of describing falconry furniture that is not directly applicable to the subject matter of the book as it varies not at all from that employed with any other falcon. The criteria remain the same. Where there are one or two differences, subtle or otherwise, which I have found may help, then these will be included in the text where appropriate. If this sounds like a copout by the author from an awful chore then it most certainly is, to which I will readily admit. Having already gone through this exercise twice in previous books, in which to be fair the information was in fact relevant, I have no intention of repeating the exercise in any form of effort to merely to pad the book out. It goes without saying that I feel from the reader's point of view surely such descriptions of falconry furniture are equally tedious to read and take up pages that could be far more usefully employed on other things. There is a very good chance that because of the subject of this book then the vast majority of falconers reading it will have a more than fundamental knowledge of the equipment required and the manner in which it is employed. If not then it is easily referenced elsewhere, an example being my own book entitled "Hunting with Aplomado Falcons".

What I do want to stress with very great emphasis is that I do not in any way what so ever condone the taking of a passage falcon under any other way than in a manner which is completely and utterly legally. Every illegal act committed in the name of falconry must surely be another nail in its coffin and contribute, no matter how insignificantly it may appear, to its eventual demise. Falconry, for the truly dedicated, will often require sacrifice in one form or another. If the passion burns within the falconer to fly a passage falcon, and to do so is not legal where the reader currently lives, then move or take an extended stay somewhere where it is possible to do so legally. I fully realise that for the vast majority this statement will be totally unrealistic, but for a very few then this is a possibility to consider. If all other avenues appear closed then at worst make contact with a falconer flying a passager and see if it might be possible to visit and at least get a taste of the holy grail of longwings. For those with an eye to appreciate such things then the effort expended will certainly be rewarded.

It is all too easy for falconers of my generation to look back with rose coloured glasses as to how things used to be and let the mists of time colour everything so that our memories focus on the good things and selectively weed out the bad. Some forty five years ago there was no domestic production of hawks and accordingly every hawk flown by a falconer was taken from the wild. Passage and unfortunately occasionally haggards were the staple stock the falconer drew from and eyass hawks were something of an exception if anything other than Sparrowhawks, Kestrels, Merlins and Buzzards. Some licences were still being issued for eyass Peregrines in the United Kingdom but these were few and far between. The vast majority of falcons were imported from Asia, Africa and the Middle East and were normally taken on migration.

Adverts would appear in various periodicals, including such oddities as "Exchange and Mart", for all sorts of weird and wonderful species, the vast majority of which had absolutely no place in falconry what so ever. Species such as White Eyed Kestrels and Black Winged Kites were commonly offered for sale. Although Sakers, Luggers, Lanners and Red Headed Merlins were relatively freely available Peregrines remained a great deal more difficult to obtain, especially in decent condition. It has to be said that some of the practices carried out with regard to trapping and shipping of raptors were nothing less than disgraceful and it was most certainly a good thing that this was gradually legislated against and, with regard to Europe at least, put an end to. I myself have ordered Lugger Falcons from India and when the box arrived at Heathrow found five Lugger Falcons so gummed up with bird lime that they had to be housed in an aviary and moulted out before they could eventually be trained and flown. Being treated in this manner not only damages the plumage of the falcons but also their outlook on life in general and man in particular. To train a falcon that has been subjected to such vile treatment is never going to go well and rarely if ever ends up with a successful hunting companion. Even more disconcertingly in the box were also two Red Headed Merlins and a Kestrel. Apparently these had been put in for the Luggers to eat if they got hungry.

Needless to say the trappers had absolutely no regard for long term conservation and although any order to a hawk dealer, in those times, would stress repeatedly that only immature falcons were wanted and adult falcons would not be accepted, what you got was always going to be an unknown quantity. So although the supply of hawks to the general falconry community dried up for a while, when this trade was outlawed here in the UK and most of Europe, the general consensus amongst falconers was that it was a good thing for the wild populations. Domestic production of hawks didn't take too long to fill the void and certainly within ten years there was no shortage of hawks and falcons for the serious falconer. Adaptations had to be made in some cases as to what species were flown and at what quarries but this was a small price to pay for the general well being of the endangered wild populations.

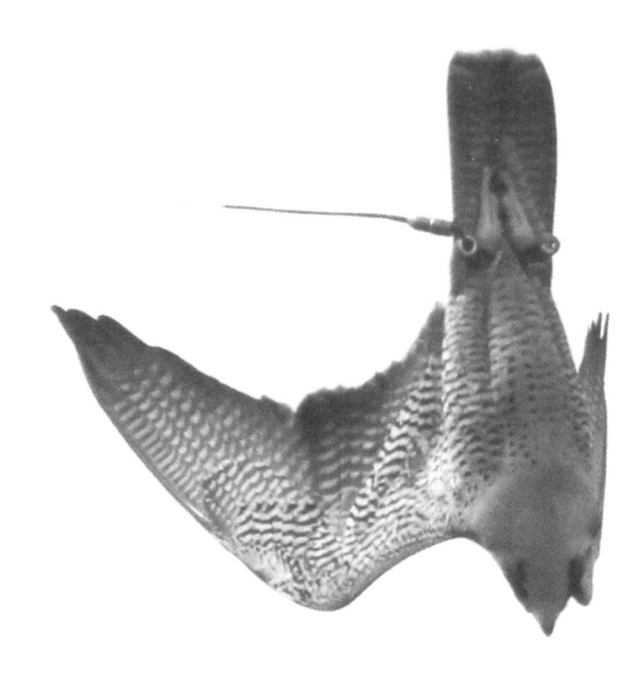

Falcon in stoop

However at a stroke it did mean that overnight the passage falcon was more or less a thing of the past. Older school falconers had to adapt their training methods and re-think to some extent the way they did things. I would most assuredly rather have a domestically produced eyass Peregrine as opposed to no Peregrine at all, but it doesn't stop me remembering how things used to be and some of the fabulous falcons that have gone before. It is a very true saying that you don't tend to appreciate what you have got until it is gone. I must admit however to having to chuckle to myself when recognised experts in the bird of prey world, as opposed to falconry one, stand up and say there is absolutely no difference between a wild falcon and a domestically produced one. To a very large extent this may be true of eyass falcons, but it hardly applies to a passager and to those that would hold this belief to be true I am afraid it only goes to prove that they have no personal experience of real falconry to draw on and with which to make a realistic and meaningful comparison. In fact it could be argued the more they pontificate on such subjects the more they clearly illustrate their lack of real knowledge. Isn't it another true saying that "an empty vessel makes the most noise". Problem is it is often these empty vessels that the authorities turn to for advice when considering new legislation regarding raptors and falconry.

In falconry terms the passage falcon is, without doubt and in the right hands, a pearl beyond price to be cherished and enjoyed. But enjoyed as she should be, that is on the wing hunting. Most passage falcons will end up lost sooner or later, as it is the nature of the falcon to press home her attack and if she fails immediately seek out another potential quarry. This is almost inevitably the outcome of a partnership between falconer and passager. However what happens before loss should produce the very highest class falconry and make the pain of loss bearable. If I can shamelessly paraphrase an old saying, then it is "better to have flown and lost a passager than never flown one at all".

Let me just finally stress that any falconer wanting to fly a passage falcon should ensure that they do so completely legally and that by their actions they do nothing to tarnish the reputation of one of the finest field sports there is. Also, and of equal importance, ensure when required that the appropriate quarry licence is in place and that seasons are adhered to. It should go without saying that a falconer should strive to carry out his or her sport in an irreproachable manner and should never under any circumstances put a stain, no matter how small, on the character of a sport that has been around for over four thousand years.

This book does not in any way claim or set out to be the definitive work on training and flying passage falcons. It is rather one person's opinion on how things are done by himself through knowledge distilled from over practically a lifetime of being fortunate to have been involved in the wonderful sport that is falconry. In many respects I prefer not to follow the paths laid down in print by falconers who, in their day, were the absolute masters of their craft and overall probably forgot more than I would ever aspire to know. That does not mean

I slavishly followed what they had set down but rather altered my ways as I learned from personal experience. Two prime examples being Edmund Bert on hooding a hawk and Gilbert Blaine on exercising a falcon to the lure.

Personally I never ever place tit bits in the hood with any hawk as encouragement to allow me to put it on her. Far rather take extra time and trouble and teach her to accept the hood without having to resort to trickery. Nor do I ever under any circumstances feed a hawk through the hood. Both I think are wrong and almost inevitably lead to a hawk that will pull and bite at the glove, when hooded, in an effort to find food. I once had the displeasure of walking the moors for the afternoon in search of Grouse with a falcon that was frequently fed through the hood. The entire afternoon, other than when it was her turn to fly, she was busy trying to bite her way through the glove in order to get something to eat. The only time she stopped was when she had finally been fed up. Hawking is supposed to pleasurable for all concerned and her biting the glove was far from pleasant for me and it must be horrendously frustrating for her if she thought she was going to find a meal by continually worrying the glove.

When it comes to stooping a falcon to the lure, I never present the lure on the ground to the falcon and then whip it away at the last minute. To me this is tantamount to teasing the falcon and can also lead to her having an accident as she tries to grab it so close to the ground. Also she will always come into the lure at full pace even if in your mind the exercise has finished and she can now have the lure and its reward. The falcon will still come into it hard and grab it with an impetus that is almost willing her to fly on with it. Not something I would ever want to encourage. Accordingly I stoop a falcon to the lure encouraging her to make passes in the air and when I have decided she has had enough I shout and throw the lure out on the ground. When she sees me do this she knows it is hers without fail and comes in at a far more reasonable pace and tends to land a great deal more gently on it.

As mentioned previously such things are not laid down by me as the only way of doing things, I would like to think I am not as arrogant as to even suggest that, but I do state these things, in my experience, work well for me and the falcons I have had the pleasure of guiding. I would hope that this book gives some insight into training passage falcons and also a degree of pleasure to those that read it. Whether or not the writing and thoughts contained in it are to your liking or not thank you for taking the time to read it and I wish you well in your falconry endeavours.

LIFE STAGES OF A FALCON

Terminology regarding the various stages of life of a falcon is somewhat open to individual interpretation and I do not think it is possible for any one person to categorically state, other than in the most obvious examples such as with a haggard, that they are one hundred per cent right. Unfortunately a very great deal of the rich and colourful language of falconry is not written down and is generally passed on from one falconer to another. Accordingly should an erroneous piece of information get taken on board it is all too easy for it, after a generation or two, to become considered a fact. Also slang terms have a horrible habit of creeping into everyday language and are used by an ever growing number who just seem incapable of referring to things with any proper title or indeed, in my opinion, a degree of merited respect. Perhaps the most common example of this dreadful abuse of language and falconry itself is referring to Peregrine falcons as Perri's or Perry's. I am afraid that personally I find it extremely offensive to show such scant regard for such magnificent creatures as Peregrine falcons by shortening their proper name to such an idiotic and completely meaningless abbreviation. It smacks to me of some of the general disregard for the lore and tradition of the magnificent field sport that is falconry that seems to be currently prevalent in quite a number of new comers to the sport, particularly so, I am sad to say, in the UK itself. This lack of respect for the tradition of falconry goes hand in hand in with another attribute that the modern hawker, can't bring myself to refer to them as falconers, seems to find an essential element of owning a hawk, camouflage clothing. The minute I see a photo of a so called falconer dressed from head to toe in camouflage clothing I have a tendency not to take that person too seriously. Falconry is not stalking or advanced survival training, so I personally fail to see the need for the supposed falconer to do their best to appear invisible, where as in actual fact their dress renders them anything but. Wearing camouflaged clothing is only effective when the wearer is keeping still and I can see no practical use for it when flying hawks at rabbits let alone a falcon at rooks. I even know of one person who flies hawks that has a camouflage patch on their glove and are proud of the fact they have a camouflaged flask for their coffee. Someone really is going to have to explain that one to me in terms of it assisting him with his falconry.

In the United Kingdom, falconry seems to mushrooming as a hobby but not as a field sport. By that I mean a large number of new comers have no interest in the history regarding the sport nor any feeling for the tradition that usually accompanies it. So many seem just hell bent on getting a Harris Hawk and bashing as many bunnies as is possible with the least amount of effort. Now I know it goes without saying that you cannot make all encompassing and sweeping generalisations because there will always be those that do care about their sport and conduct themselves in a thoroughly sporting manner. However, because I supplied falconry equipment as part of my means of earning my living for more than twenty five years, I probably come into contact with a great many more new comers to the sport than the average falconer. I would have to say that I find these individuals on a regular basis to be very depressing when it comes to the future of the sport. I have recently had to find homes for seven Harris Hawks and three falcons that had all been brought more or less on a whim and then discarded when things didn't seem quite as easy in real life as when read about in a book, or viewed as a small clip in the midst of a block buster on the big screen.

Most falconers would, I think, tend to agree that a falcon has seven separate life stages, although the names of these various stages can differ from area to area and country to country. For those with a keen interest in the history of falconry they will correctly argue that there are in fact eight life stages for a falcon but one of which is so obscure and only ever referred to in the vaguest of terms that, personally, I do not use it and know of no one else that does so. This term is Lenten Hawk, which refers to a young falcon that has reached her first Christmas but has not yet started the process of the first moult. As I say it is a term I have only read of in old falconry books and have never heard any falconer make mention of it. Accordingly I will record here the seven stages as I have always understood them and note the one or two alternative names that are relatively common in both their usage and understanding. For those studying the subject of falconry it should always be remembered that it is human nature to almost automatically believe what appears in print, especially if the publication concerned is from antiquity, and therefore misdirection can so easily be passed from generation to generation completely unintentionally. A classic example of this would be the Mews. This word is now in general usage as a term for the place where hunting hawks are housed and sleep on a day to day basis. The term is the correct one for a place where hawks are turned loose to moult and hawk house is the proper term for day to day quarters. However usage, or rather incorrect usage, over several generations now means the term Mews is generally used for day to day housing and modern falconers can point to certain publications to try and prove they are using the term correctly. Am I being pedantic in my desire to see the correct terminology used in the sport I hold dear? No I don't think so, any language is only kept alive by its constant use and it is important this usage is accurate as well as completely correct in context.

Haggard Falcon

For the average falconer in his day to day discussions then only the three most common terms will probably come up in conversation, these being eyass, passage and haggard. Where sometimes confusion can arise is when it comes to discussing falcons that have been moulted in captivity. It is as if with changing her feathers the falcon has somehow or another changed her origins and passed from one stage to another, which of course just simply isn't the case. For example, a falcon taken on passage and then intermewed three times is a passage falcon in her fourth season. She hasn't suddenly become a haggard simply because she has swathed herself in the cloak of adulthood. She remains, and always will do so, what she was when she came into the life of the falconer, that is a passage falcon. An eyass falcon can moult as many times as it likes, I have an eyass Peregrine Falcon here that is in her late teens, but she will remain an eyass for her entire life.

It goes without saying really that the first stage in the life of any falcon, in terms of its relevance to falconry, is of course, the egg, which has been laid in the eyrie. Whereas the aviculturist will refer to the moment that a chick emerges from the egg as hatching the falconer will use the term disclosed to cover the same event. Accordingly what is then a simple chick to the aviculturist starts the transformation from egg to falcon through its various guises for the falconer.

Having been disclosed the contents of the egg become stage two, the Eyas. The word eyas, which can also be spelt correctly as eyass, comes from the old French word "Niais" meaning a nest. Many falconers refer to any nestling falcon, no matter what the stage of development providing the youngster is still in the eyrie, as an eyas. This really isn't correct. We are talking wild falcons here at the nest site, not captive reared falcons on an artificial nest ledge in an aviary.

Once the eyas becomes somewhat mobile and can start to move about on the ledge where the eyrie is sited she moves into stage three of her development and becomes a Ramager. This is around the third week of her life approximately and at first movement will verge on the comical. The falcon will most likely shuffle around on her tarsi, the long lower part of her leg. Eventually her strength and sense of balance will develop sufficiently that she is able, somewhat unsteadily, to walk around upright on her feet. The sense of inquisitiveness will not take her far, merely a few paces, and she will constantly return to the hub of the eyrie. Ramager is a term that has always more or less been used solely when referring to young peregrines and doesn't really apply to other species of falcon. It is also a term that is rarely used nowadays and will probably slip away from useage altogether unless care is taken.

A week or ten days or so of this limited movement will see strength and a sense of balance and awareness develop in the young falcon and so we move

Eyass Aplomado Falcons

into the next stage of her life cycle which is that of the brancher. Generally considered a term only truly applicable to hawks raised in a nest, brancher does also rightly refer to the eyass falcon tentatively exploring the nest ledge. She is now being provided with a good growth of feathers, although a great deal of down is still present. In the case of European Peregrine Falcons it should now be the first or second week of June, providing all went well with the first clutch, however there are many factors that can contribute to this ideal schedule being put out of kilter. Varying degrees of food availability, weather conditions, predation and sickness as well as a host of other possible influences can all have a bearing on things running according to nature's general plan.

After a month or so of branching, where strength and co-ordination of the falcon increases, feather growth completes its mission and muscle starts to build from the constant flapping exercises the falcon indulges in on a very regular basis, it comes time to leave the safety of the eyrie for long periods of time. These periods will be extended each day until eventually the eyrie is used purely as a place to home back to and sleep, or more correctly jowke, in the vicinity of. The young falcon has now not only left the nest but is receiving constant hunting lessons from its parents and is starting to make kills for itself. Before too long the parents of the young falcons raised at the eyrie will be encouraging it, quite forcibly sometimes, to leave and start fending for themselves completely. It is now that we move on to a very important stage in the life of a young falcon from a falconer's point of view. The youngster now becomes a Red Hawk or, a term hardly used nowadays and when it is, as often as not, it is used incorrectly, a Falcon Gentle. This term is often thought to indicate a Peregrine Falcon at any stage in life and is merely an alternative name for such. It is strictly speaking only applicable to a young falcon that has left the nest and is starting to fend for itself up to the point where it embarks on its first passage.

This is a time in a falcon's life that medieval falconers used to love to take their falcons from the wild and some of the very top longwing falconers in Mexico, for example, still continue to do so. The falcon has severed its family ties, is killing for itself, has learnt to use the wind and its own powers of flight to good effect but has not yet set off on migration. Any such falcon taken by a competent falconer will be free of vices such as mantling and screaming but will be young enough to slightly re-educate in the service of man without tremendous trauma on the part of the falcon or, come to that, the falconer. Many eyries become firm favourites with falconers and the youngsters they produce are what a falconer looks for when it comes time to replace a member of the team.

One of my friends in Mexico, who flies a team of three peregrine Falcons at duck, always tries to get Red Hawks from a particular eyrie. He believes that the high rocky outcrop of the location of the eyrie helps to produce youngsters that have to very quickly learn how to deal with up draughts and down draughts efficiently or simply not survive. Whatever the truth of the thinking behind this reasoned argument is makes no difference. The point is the falconer believes it and thereby works with the falcon feeling exceedingly confident as to the eventual outcome. This confidence means his whole approach to working with the young falcon is completely positive and forward looking, which has got to be the right way to approach things. Whether or not there is logic to his thinking doesn't really matter, he fully believes it and his confidence exudes into his working with the falcon.

With the approach of winter we move onto the sixth stage in the life of a falcon when she starts to migrate and becomes a Passage Falcon. This is the jewel in the crown of falconry, particularly a passage falcon that is taken in January or February. The young falcon has now left the eyrie far behind some six months or so ago and has been living totally independently for all but a week or two of that time when her parents still provided the occasional meal. She has learnt to deal with the elements and has honed her hunting prowess. She is very obviously a successful falcon or she would not have reached this stage in her life. To be on passage means she is strong, well developed and at the height of her powers. Migration is an arduous undertaking for any avian species and the fact that she was on passage means she feels well, is confident and happy to undertake such a potentially taxing journey. Any falconer who has ever had such a wondrous falcon as a true passager come into his or her possession will know that they have, in falconry terms, a pearl beyond price. Something to be savoured and have the ultimate care and consideration applied when working with her. That is not to say any falcon, at no matter what life stage, should not have the utmost care taken with her, but with the passager, the bond between her and falconer is always a very tenuous one and extra care needs to be lavished on her. Truly, in my opinion, the training of a passage falcon sorts the serious falconer from the not quite so fully committed (or some would say fanatical).

But surely to be a good falconer and to show quality sport in a consistent manner does take quite a serious degree of something bordering on obsession. Most true falconers strive to obtain the very best flights for their falcons that they can. They don't do it for the satisfaction of others but to see a falcon fly and hunt at the best or her ability and in pursuit of a quarry that tests her and the falconer's field craft to the full. It is a very old saying and all will have heard it countless times, but it loses nothing of its truth content for all of that. "Nothing is better as a field sport than good falconry, poor falconry is a travesty". With the passage falcon the falconer starts with a completely clean sheet and with a falcon that has a very definite advantage over an eyass or falcon gentle. How good that falcon will turn out in terms of falconry will be a measure of good he or she is in having empathy with the falcon and truly understanding dietary and other needs of the raptor. A passage falcon takes a knowledgeable falconer to get the best from it and will not in itself make up for any shortfall on the part of the falconer.

The final life stage of the falcon is when it has moulted in the wild for the first time and it then becomes a haggard. Normally in these present times a wild falcon is considered a haggard once it has more or less completed the moult and has become a blue falcon. In days gone by our forefathers considered the young falcon had turned into a haggard as soon as any blue feathers started to show through. The reasoning for this was, the fact that the falcon had started to moult meant she has completed her first passage successfully and therefore moved on in her life. Either way makes complete sense and most of the haggard peregrines I have ever flown have been blue falcons when they came into my possession. A haggard is not something I have ever deliberately set out to own, even in the days when wild taken falcons could legally be flown in Britain, even though they had to initially be taken somewhere else, usually Pakistan or India.

The reasons for not wanting a haggard are blatantly obvious but I will none the less state them. Firstly from a conservation point of view the haggard falcon is potential breeding stock and should be left where it is. The fact that it has survived to true adult hood means it is strong and has the right genetic make up that should be passed on to who knows how many future offspring. Wild populations of any avian species, but particularly in the case of predatory ones, can fluctuate dramatically at any time and therefore good breeding stock should be left in the wild where it undoubtedly belongs. From a falconry point of view the haggard falcon has spent several years fending admirably for herself and has developed her own style of hunting with her own preferences as to method of attack and favourite quarry species. It is highly unlikely that these will coincide with the hopes and desires of the falconer. Haggard peregrines in the wild will often take, given the right set of circumstances, Corvids of various species, but in a trained capacity they will normally have be flown in a reduced condition to get them to fly them with any degree of enthusiasm. What falconer can ever look at a falcon he is flying which has no bloom on its feathers, no colour in its cere or feet, no sparkle in its eye without feeling, quite rightly, a great deal of shame. Better not to fly such a falcon at a particular quarry if the only way to get it to partake in the branch of falconry you want it to follow is to reduce it so drastically. This is without giving any consideration to the effect to what flying a falcon so reduced in condition will have on its long term health.

I have flown several haggards but these have been for rehabilitation purposes. Although fun to train and fly, because of the challenge they initially seemed to represent, the sooner they could be "cast downwind to prey at fortune" the better. Haggards, like passage falcons, tend to have extremely good manners and, for those that know how to do so properly, are very good to the hood. Getting a haggard to come to a lure on a creance is a very different kettle of fish to getting one to return to the very same lure after an unsuccessful flight at quarry. It is also a thing of wonder as to just how quickly a beautifully mannered haggard, that weathered so calmly on the falconers lawn a couple of hours previously, can turn into a distrusting nervous falcon wary of both the lure and the falconer after an unsuccessful flight. I well remember a haggard not too long ago that I was rehabilitating and everyone that saw her marvelled at her good manners, calm demeanour and general gentleness. This same falcon came into the lure after an unsuccessful flight at rook and as I bent down giving her tit bits as she ate from the lure I suddenly sneezed violently. She instantly stepped back from the lure, looked at me wild eyed and took off and it took me several hours to initially track her down. She moved and had to be re-located seven times before she eventually being left out overnight. The following day she finally came into the lure having moved and been relocated several times more. If it wasn't for the fact that I knew her fitness wasn't one hundred per cent at that time I would have left her to her own devices. She was exceedingly nervous to pick up off of the lure and took several days to get back to where we had been before the sneezing episode.

I suppose one of the biggest differences between the modern falconer and his predecessors is that nowadays we have the benefit of telemetry when flying our falcons. I can only assume our forefathers would have had to have cut their falcons quite a bit harder in condition to get the sort of response from them that they were looking for than the modern falconer would. Allied to this would be the fact they would not have had the benefit of scales as we do now and take so readily for granted. For them all judgements with regard to flying were based on pinching the breast of the falcon, surely the most inaccurate way ever of judging the condition of a falcon, and the seasoned eye of the falconer coupled with the responses in the falcon itself. In the case of the haggard falcon where so often the calm, placid and amenable falcon on the weathering ground would transform to an almost wild falcon once more when back in the field goes a long way to explaining why falconers from previous generations were reluctant to expend time and energy training them.

Flying passage falcons without the aids, such as scales and telemetry, that the modern falconer now takes for granted must have meant that flying them was always a true adventure as the outcome was so precariously in the balance as to the recovery of the falcon, never mind being successful at quarry. It is so often argued as to whether or not falconers from times gone by were more skilled than the modern falconer and even if the golden days of falconry are long gone. But such comparisons are meaningless because each generation learns by what is the considered norm at the time. I myself flew for a number of years where telemetry was simply not available. When I did finally have access to a set, what a revelation it was. However, unlike with an eyass, telemetry was just an aid to recovery not a means with a very high expected success rate. With that I mean that there are those, principally flying eyas falcons, which take risks they wouldn't take if they didn't have telemetry to help them in a recovery if required. As with so many things in life telemetry used well is an excellent aid, but it is that, an aid and not a solution in itself.

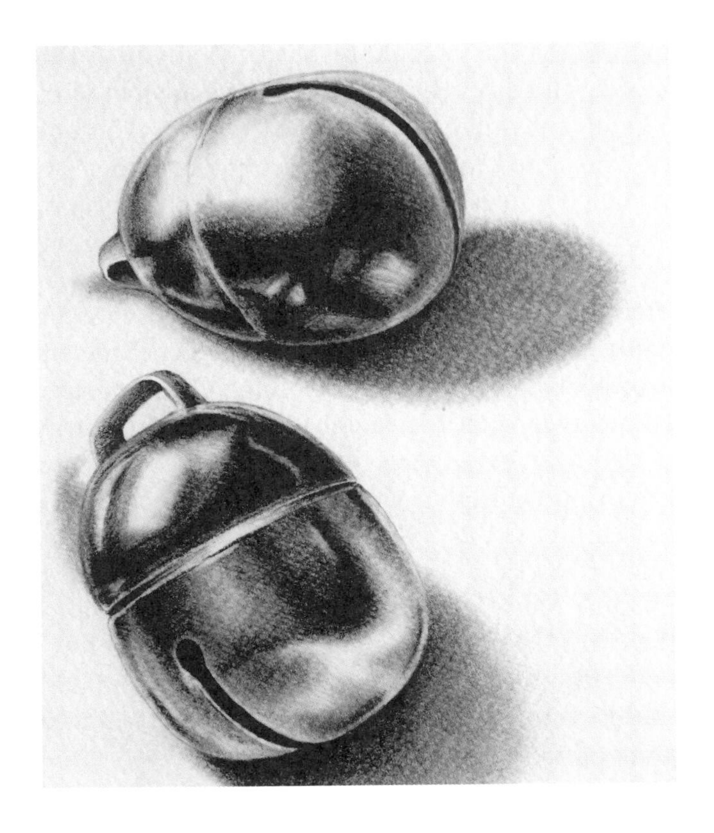

EQUIPMENT

As with any falcon, regardless of size, equipment fitted to the passage falcon needs to be as light and as strong as possible yet still be completely practical. Everything else used in connection with the falcon needs to be of the very highest quality. As I stated in my book on Aplomado Falcons I am often reminded of a couple of old maxims when it comes to talking about falconry equipment and they are “you get what you pay for in life” and “if you can’t afford to do it properly then don’t do it”. Nowadays in the somewhat degenerate times in which we find ourselves, such sayings are probably considered quaint and almost archaic. None the less however, they still are both very true, apt and utterly relevant to the matter in hand. I still find it staggering when I look at falconry magazines or on social media sites that someone has taken the trouble to obtain an absolute pearl of a falcon and yet decks it out in the cheapest falconry furniture available and adds insult to injury by perching it on some form of self made contraption that I would be reluctant to use as firewood. Do these people really not see what they are doing and do they not have sufficient pride in what they do that they would be happy in anything less than the very best for their hawks. The difference in price between what will, at an absolute push, do in an emergency and the very finest falconry furniture available is negligible when considered in the overall scheme of things. Added to this of course is the fact that if you use the very best of the falconry furniture available you will have peace of mind as your falcon sits weathering on her block and not be worrying that a swivel will break and she will be away to an almost inevitable miserable death somewhere. Also if hooded with a decent hood in the company of other falcons she will not get the hood off and either do damage to other falcons or be damaged herself. If nothing else then surely pride on the part of the falconer will want his falcon decked out in the best equipment even if no one else ever gets to see it or appreciate it. There is a sense of satisfaction when using the best of what is available and it is also aesthetically pleasing. It is not as if those that fly passage falcons are ever going to be flying a multiple or stud of hawks and if they do find themselves in such a position then I would imagine their financial circumstances would allow for the best equipment. Either way, the passage falcon is special in that it is a fact that will have to be accepted, that she will bate more than an eyass in the early days and is accordingly deserving of the finest, if only to satisfy the falconers concerns from a safety point of view.

If we start our look at equipment with what the falcon herself wears then the logical place to start will be with jesses. I use kangaroo, either veg (vegetable) tan or natural, keeping the thickness of the skin as low as is still compatible with good strength. The actual anklets I use are half an inch wide and two inches long for a tiercel and five eights of an inch wide and two and three eights of an inch long for a falcon. The eyelet size I prefer to use is size 22 for both sexes although most people use 22 for the tiercel and 24 for the falcon. The mews jesses are some five inches long and three eights of an inch wide for the tiercel and half an inch wide and six inches long for the falcon. In the early days of flying loose I use field jesses which are slightly longer and thinner than the mews jesses. But as soon as I have the full confidence of the hawk I do away with flying jesses as quickly as possible. I have never found that larger passage falcons seem to suffer with the trait sometimes seen in trained accipiters of clutching anything that dangles close to their feet whilst in flight but why present the opportunity, and therefore the possible temptation, if you don't have to. This can be so frustrating when trying to exercise the falcon or, worse still, when entering it. With some falcons as soon as they feel the field jess dangling they grab it and then their attention is not focused on what they should be doing but rather a leather strap clutched for dear life in their foot. With care and attention to manning and all other stages of training the use of field jesses should only be required in the early days of flying, and this will be to serve more as a confidence booster for the falconer than any real practical requirement. Although it must be said some falcons are always tricky to pick up and can continue to be so throughout their career. I have a six times intermewed falcon that I would never fly without field jesses as it is highly excitable when first taken back up onto the fist. It is perfectly obedient to the lure and will jump from the lure to the fist, but once there as often as not would prefer to be somewhere else. Flying jesses means there isn't a mad scramble on my part to get the falcon safely clipped back onto the glove.

To fit the anklets I use a plier type tool and, as stated, size 22 eyelets. The pliers themselves have nice small heads and are simple and straightforward to use, one good squeeze and the male and female parts of the eyelet are well and truly closed. Size 22 eyelets are small enough to be nice and neat and large enough to get suitable soft leather jesses through without too much friction. Jesses and other bits and pieces of leather equipment will need to be kept greased and I have found Ko-Cho-Line grease to be about the best for my needs. It does the job well, is easily absorbed by the leather and does not make it feel slimy. It is reasonably priced and a tin will last the average falconer a very long time. There are also false aylmeri anklets which really are very quick and simple to use and mean that the falconer can, quite literally, change the anklets in a matter of seconds. The argument against false aylmeri anklets is that older patterns would leave the tongue containing the eyelet very proud of the hawk's leg and therefore perhaps provide the makings of an accident. With today's better design the whole arrangement is light yet strong and sits as close to the falcon's leg as a conventional anklet system would.

When it comes to swivels then please, especially if you have any respect for your falcon, only ever use properly custom designed and made falconry swivels. The vast majority are made from stainless steel and there are even some made in titanium. Do not under any circumstances be tempted to use cheap mass produced swivels that cost a matter of pence as opposed to pounds. They are not produced to help prevent a bating falcon from flying off and are cheap because they are low quality material and mass production techniques used to make them. You will see plenty on offer at country fairs and on internet auction sites. Do not be tempted ever to use with a falcon. They are probably acceptable as swivels on lures lines but not very much else. I personally have known of three falcons and two hawks that have bated and broken such swivels, snapping them as if they were twigs. Fortunately in all five cases the hawks and falcons were recovered but what if this had not been the case. The possible resulting Nor do I ever use dog lead swivels. I am fully aware of those that use the argument that if this type of swivel is strong enough to hold a dog then it will certainly be strong enough for a falcon. My view on the subject is that should a dog swivel break when restraining a dog it is going to be when the owner or handler is in attendance and therefore they will be in a situation where they can instantly rectify the accident. Should this type of swivel be used with a falcon, then it is most likely to fail when the falcon is weathering and therefore may be in a situation where it bates occasionally putting extra pressure on an already questionable item. A falcon that goes off with its legs tethered together can only ever have a miserable outcome to its life. What if such an item where to be used and fail in the hawk house where other falcons are kept. The possible consequences once again really don't bear thinking about. Anyone contemplating the use of such items can only be doing so from the point of view of saving financial outlay and if that is the case then I would urge that falconry really isn't the sport for such an individual.

Passage Falcon under anesthetic for coping

Of the three designs of modern falconry swivels, that is D shape, flat top and figure of eight, I far prefer the flat top design for my personal use. This is simply because I find that the flat top really does seem to prevent the jesses slipping down the main body of the swivel and thereby stop the swivel doing its basic job. For the larger falcons I am also a great admirer of the modified Sampo swivel as I find them superb at preventing jesses twisting and they are immensely strong. Sampo swivels seem to be the falconry equivalent of "Marmite", you either love them or hate them. I have heard so many stories over the years of this type of swivel breaking but have yet to meet anyone it has actually happened to. Most people seem to have heard horror stories concerning them but have not actually had instances that they personally know to be true. I have used them for many years and American falconers use little else. If you understand the construction of a Sampo swivel then you will soon realise it is virtually impossible for it to come apart. If it fails then it fails in the respect of being able to rotate and therefore act as a swivel anymore. This will be picked up immediately by the falconer and a replacement can be affected. Again I have never had this happen to me or know anyone it has happened to.

For leashes I make mine from eight plait five mm matt polyester and they are some sixty inches in length. At one end a figure of eight knot is tied and the top of the arrangement is then heated with a naked flame until it welds into a strong and neat finish. A leather washer has a hole in its centre only just sufficiently large enough to pass the leash through is then run up to the knotted end till it butts up to it. The outer circumference of the washer should be approximately the same diameter as the knot itself. This is simply a wear washer to help prevent the metal of the swivel constantly rubbing up against the underside of the knot. The end of the leash that passes through the lower ring of the swivel will also have its end neatly sealed by the use of heat. This helps prevent the leash end from fraying and becoming a mess.

Despite my careful outlining of well known and commonly used jess, swivel, leash arrangement above I have in fact myself now switched almost entirely to the so called "Bullet Jess" system where jesses, leash and swivel are an all in one arrangement with the ends of the jesses having a small metal bar, very much in the shape of a bullet at their end, which is where the systems gets its name from, and this bullet is passed through the eyelet on the anklet. The bar, having passed through the eyelet, now sits sideways against the eyelet and is all but impossible to get back through the eyelet unless intentionally positioned and helped through by the falconer. This means that when in the field the whole arrangement can be removed in seconds. With a new falcon or one that tends to be restless on the fist, either permanent field jesses can be attached to the anklet or normal flying jesses fitted at the time of flying. There are many different sets on the market and yet again I must make the point that you get what you pay for. Made from cheaper materials the jess part of the system goes hard quite quickly and is then very prone to tangling. Pay slightly more, get better quality and have a much less stress free time worrying as to whether or not the swivel part of the all in one arrangement is working properly.

Personally I don't tend to fit bells and bewits to my falcons anymore as telemetry is now so sophisticated and reliable. Also of course, transmitters are continually getting smaller and more powerful and with the ability to back pack now, the most sensible way of mounting a transmitter to a larger falcon. Even for the falconer that loves the tradition of falconry, the question that will inevitably come to mind sooner or later is "do bells have a place anymore". Certainly there are occasions when the bell is still an excellent tool, such as with a falcon that has killed a grouse in long heather or a peat hag, or perhaps a rook in a root field. Telemetry will give a pretty accurate direction but a tinkling bell will quickly give an exact location. Where a bell is undeniably still a very useful tool is when applied to the home life of a falcon. When close at hand but actually out of sight the bell gives the falconer a pretty accurate indication of what his falcon or falcons are doing. The rapid tinkling in short bursts means a falcon is scratching and attending to her plumage. The muffled series of dull tinkles means she is enjoying a bath. The constant harsh ring means she is bating and should stop as quickly as it has begun. If not then the falconer needs to quickly check on his charges. There are some very good quality bells around with a tone and ring quality that will carry a very good distance. Ironically I tend to fit at least one bell to my falcons at home by means of a button bewit so I can take it off when we go out to the field. So very different to years ago, when the bell would be removed at home but slavishly fitted before heading out to the field. For those that are going to fit bells then the traditional bewit is obviously the best tool for the job if the bells are to be left on the falcon at all times. For ease of slipping on and off then probably the button bewit is ideal for the job. Under no circumstances what so ever cable tie a bell to the anklet of the falcon or worse to the leg of the falcon itself. This lazy and thoughtless method I have seen far too many times to be comfortable with and unfortunately sufficiently enough to give me concern as to the general standard of modern falconry. The second is truly horrendous and there is no possible excuse what so ever for its usage other than ignorance and or laziness. The potential for a serious accident is all too obvious for me to even bother mentioning. No genuine falconer would ever do this or be a party to such a travesty.

When it comes to hoods my own personal preference is for a blocked Dutch hood but with an American style opening. In other words I want my falcons, should the need arise, to be able to cast or be sick whilst wearing the hood and minimise the possibility of the falcon choking. Older, true Dutch hoods, were relatively heavy affairs and had a letter box style opening as opposed to the well shaped key hole style of today. The modern version of the Dutch hood is a much more comfortable affair for a falcon to wear, providing the aperture is cut correctly and doesn't have an edge rubbing against the soft skin of the falcon's mandible. When it comes to weight there is practically no difference between a Dutch, Anglo Indian or Bahraini style of hood. It really does come down to the personal preference of the falconer and also which hood the falcon is comfortable in. If a falcon constantly scratches at a hood then logic will tell you she is not comfortable in it and you need to ensure it is not touching somewhere it shouldn't or it is letting light in, which will drive a falcon to distraction. Gortex braces are now very much the order of the day for all hoods and they won't seize and bind together should they inadvertently get soaked as was always the case when leather braces were used. A hood holder on the belt or shoulder strap of the hawking vest is a very useful item and will keep the hood from being accidently misshapen by being stuffed into a pocket or worse still lost when running after the falcon in the field.

For a creance I use fifty metres of R18 natural polyester line wound in the traditional figure of eight method onto a turned stick of approximately nine inches long. Both ends of the stick have been nicely rounded and smoothed on a wood lathe and the stick has a small hole drilled through the centre of it equal distance from each end. The creance line is passed through this hole and then tied back to itself to prevent it ever slipping back through the hole. In this way the line will always remain attached to the stick and any hawk that makes off with the full length of the creance will have the stick acting as a drag and consequently arresting its progress. The end of the line that is to be used for attaching to the hawk will be sealed with heat just as with the end of leashes. I do not put any form of clip on the end of my creance lines as I never ever attach a creance to any hawk by any other means than the falconers knot. I think that the use of clips is inviting an accident and for the same reason I always remove the swivel from the falcon and attach the creance line to the slits in the mews jesses. The thought process behind this is that the leather slit will be the weakest part of the arrangement. If the condition of the hawk has been misjudged and she tries to rake away it is the jess slit that will take any brunt. With decent jesses this will not pose a problem but should there be any weak link this will be it. It can be bad enough having a hawk prematurely loose without having the added worry that its legs are also handcuffed together. In any case the falconer will not normally put his falcon on the creance until he is pretty sure the outcome of the exercise will be a positive one. As we are all aware a creance is a necessary evil and the sooner it can be dispensed with the better. It may be worth mentioning that some falconers sharpen one end of the lure stick to a point so that they can drive it into the ground in the early days of training. Rather than have the stick itself act as a drag the falcon is brought up unceremoniously when she reaches the end of the line. As harsh as this may sound if the falcon is being trained where it could possibly reach some tress and therefore become tangled, by dragging the creance a relatively short distance, then very probably its use is justified.

Tiercel on Cadge and Saker Falcon on block

The lure is a very important item and one that should be given some considerable thought before the falcon is introduced to it. Sizes, weight, plain or feathered are all things to be given consideration. In fact I attach such importance to it, particularly in the case of the passage falcon, that I cover this one item of equipment very extensively in the chapter entitled "The Lure, Introduction and Calling Off". Therefore I will just touch on it very briefly here in this chapter. The lure itself is traditionally a horseshoe shaped leather bag stuffed to give the appropriate weight and feel. In the centre of the pad are two strings on each side by which means the food can be securely attached to the lure. The body of the lure has a reinforced pad at the apex end with a size 22 eyelet set into it. Through this eyelet is attached a split ring of the type used on key rings and to this split ring a normal swivel is attached. Tied to the swivel is some five yards of cotton line which itself is attached to a lure stick, normally a piece of one and a quarter inch diameter doweling some nine inches long. The use of pure cotton line is very important as it eliminates any chance of a friction burn should the lure line be required to be pulled through the hand quickly such as when stooping a falcon to the lure. The swivel at the lure end of the arrangement allows the lure itself to turn when required and therefore the line itself does not become all twisted and tangled.

I am never certain if wings really do have any relevance on a lure as surely no falcon is stupid enough to think that a lump of leather is capable of sprouting wings and flying. It is hard to break with tradition however and somehow wings being attached to a lure certainly seem to give the falconer confidence in its abilities to lure a falcon back. Obviously the wings on a lure that is used frequently will soon be very much the worse for wear and they need to be changed on a regular basis. Dried wings of the sort considered appropriate can quickly and easily be attached to the lure by means of cable ties through pre-drilled holes in the body of the lure.

The only time I don't use a particularly light lure is in the early days of training. I then use a considerable heavier one when the initial presentation of the lure to the falcon is being carried out. This is in the hopes of preventing any chance of that awful vice of carrying creeping into the proceedings. If your initial manning and eventual introduction to the lure have been done carefully and with attention to detail then the thought of attempting to carry should never enter the falcons head. But all of us can make mistakes and unforeseen circumstances can sometimes occur and scupper our well laid plans. So for the first few lessons I use a lure that looks identical to the one I shall use on a day to day basis in the near future but is packed with stones in the body and is therefore somewhat heavier.

I have never used a pole lure or any form of kite training when it comes to passage falcons. I prefer the close somewhat personal feel the traditional swung lure gives as opposed to the pole lure. In my opinion kiting serves no useful purpose in getting a passage falcon fit or teaching it about height or using the wind. So other than as a desperate last hope recall to a lost falcon I don't see any practical use of the kite that would justifiably reward the time spent teaching it to fly to it. The passage falcon, in the hands of the falconer, should not be off of the wing long enough to have lost all its fitness.

With regard to blocks I have now gone over completely to the use of plastic ones. I find them easy to clean, attractive to look at and they will withstand the rigours of more or less anything the weather can throw at them. My own preference when it comes to Peregrines is for blocks that have six inch diameter top for tiercels and an eight inch top for falcons. The top of the block will be some fifteen to twenty inches above the ground once the spike has been pushed fully home. For indoor blocks I like the same dimensions but with a heavy duty base obviously. The tops of the blocks have plastic artificial grass set into them and each block has a spare piece so as to allow cleaning. The tops of the blocks also have two drain holes drilled in them beneath the layer of artificial grass. This is to allow excess water to run cleanly away after a rain shower or cleaning.

When it comes to baths I much prefer those that are mode with sloping sides and have some raised chequering in the bottom to enable the falcon to have some grip when standing in it. Sizes that I find best are approximately twenty six inches in diameter and around three inches deep for a tiercel and thirty inches in diameter and three and half inches deep for a falcon. At a push a falcon bath will do for a tiercel but just don't fill it quite so much but a tiercel sized bath is just a little on the small side for an enthusiastic bathing falcon. Modern baths are made from fibre glass and coloured deep green. I have seen yellow and even purple baths for sale at various country fairs and I suppose they are as adequate for their purpose as any other colour, But I think it will take a great deal of persuading to move me away from traditional green.

When it comes to scales they can be of either the electronic or the conventional balance type that require a set of weights. I use both types and as long as both are accurate it doesn't really matter which ones are used. I tend to use the conventional balance scales when at home and if away hawking then take my electronic ones with me. When it comes to electronic scales then this is the one time I tend to break my own rule about buying the supposedly best that money can buy. Some of the specially adapted electronic scales that are currently on the market are indeed excellent, but the most expensive dedicated electronic falconry scales of all that I have come across are just so unreliable as to make them worse than no scales at all. I buy my scales, a decent make, from a hardware shop and fit a perch to them myself. This really is a very simple matter and the resultant affair is practical and reliable.

Casting jackets are a relatively recent addition to the list of falconry furniture required by the modern falconer and one that I think is a really worthwhile addition. These jackets are a method of restraining the hawk so as to enable to the falconer to carry out minor operations such as fitting new anklets or coping single handedly. The jacket is an oblong of material with adjustable Velcro fastenings that is passed around the body of the hawk and then secured upon itself. The hawk is effectively straight jacketed with head free at one end and legs accessible at the other. A very simple and straight forward piece of equipment to use and one that is extremely effective. Once you have got used to using one it is difficult to imagine how we ever coped single handedly without them. That is the very big advantage of these jackets, it means that jobs that normally require two people can be done effectively single handedly and not postponed until a willing or sometimes unwilling volunteer is pressed into service.

The conventional hawking bag is more or less a thing of the past now with modern falconers switching to hawking vests or custom made gilets. The latter being of more use really for occasions when the falcon is being trained or exercised to the lure as opposed to hunting when more pockets will be required for the extra equipment carried. The Hawking Vest has been developed over the years to accommodate all that the falconer requires in the field as well as a decent across the back pocket for quarry taken. The better quality vests are made from such materials as Cordura which means they are hard wearing, comfortable to wear and can be thrown in the washing machine when required.

The reason the vest has overtaken the conventional falconry bag so thoroughly is, in my opinion, the fact that everything is held against the upper body of the falconer and therefore the nightmare of getting over fences with a traditional bag swinging from the hip is a thing of the past. Also trying to run with a bag swaying somewhat irritatingly, with what seems like a mind of its own, from the hip was never a pleasant thing.

Travel boxes come in a remarkable variation of sizes and materials and some have obviously had a great deal of thought put into them and some, unfortunately, blatantly none. The purpose of a travel box is to provide a safe place of containment for the falcon to travel between destinations. Its basic requirements are that it is sufficiently large to comfortably house the intended occupant but should not be so large as to allow the falcon to fully spread its wings or to raise its tail ninety degrees. If it can do either of these things then there is a good chance that feather damage will ensue when the falcon is transported in such a box. The box should have plenty of ventilation yet remain quite dark enough inside to keep an unhooded falcon calm. Ventilation holes should be drilled in the lower portion of the box not up near the top as with so many badly thought out boxes. If the box has the holes near the top and an unhooded hawk is being travelled in it then the hawk will be restless for the entire duration of the journey, constantly striving towards the light.

The door can be fitted to open either right or left in accordance with which ever hand the falconer uses. For example most falconers are right handed and therefore carry the falcon on their left hand. For these people the box needs to open from the left hand side with the right hand side being hinged to the body of the box. Otherwise removing the falcon from the box, even if the falcon is hooded, is an awkward procedure. The box should have a decent, sturdy collapsible handle and a very secure door catch which preferably would have a backup system. This means that if the catch accidentally gets knocked the door still cannot come open unexpectedly. No fixings from the handle or the catch should intrude into the box in such a manner that they could in any way damage its occupant. A removal drain plug in the bottom of the box makes life easier but is not essential. As I only use plastic boxes then cleaning them with a power washer on a regular basis is simplicity itself. A mixture of warm water and F10 disinfectant is normally sufficient to ensure a thorough cleansing job.

The dimensions of a travelling box for a Peregrine Falcon will be as follows. The height will be twenty five inches, depth twenty inches and width will be seventeen inches. For a tiercel height will be twenty-two inches, depth eighteen inches and width fourteen and a half inches. A perch will be set across the width of the box at a height of eight inches from the floor and back eleven inches from the front. I normally use a piece of two by two and cover this with plastic artificial grass. It should be remembered that legally a travelling box is precisely that, for transporting a falcon from A to B. Not to be used as an overnight quarters when away from home. The exception to this would be when treating a sick falcon and in such a case the cross beam style perch would probably be removed and either a cut down indoor block put in or a towel or similar for the falcon to lie on.

Telemetry is without doubt the most expensive single piece of equipment the falconer will ever have to purchase. There are several very good systems on the market and several that are not rated as highly as others. Buy the best you can you afford and it will pay you back many times over. If you think about it logically, to recover one falcon with the use of your telemetry set means the system has more than paid for itself. Probably the world leader in telemetry at the moment would be Marshall, manufactured in the USA. They have reliable long range transmitters that can be switched on and off with a magnetic wand, enjoy long battery life and come in a range of strengths to suit all different aspects of hawking. Their receivers are also first class and come in a range of frequencies to suit the legal requirements of the countries they are marketed in. Ease of use and also being aesthetically pleasing are bonuses but it is the reliability and the power to inspire confidence that makes them a leader in their chosen field. However, in my opinion, very close on their heels come Luksander with their range of products. Not as easy on the eye as their rival's products they are however extremely well made, reliable and robust. The receivers they market have changed very little in appearance over the years and are somewhat clumsy in operation when compared to Marshall Products. Having said that they have never ever let me down and their products inspire confidence in me. For that reason, although I have two Marshall Receivers, I simply cannot bring myself to get rid of my old Luksander set. In fact if truth be told I personally tend to use the Marshall receiver to locate the right area when first setting out on a tracking mission then rely on the Luksander when getting close. This is no reflection on the capabilities of one set over another merely my own confidence in using a particular system.

Transmitters can be mounted in various ways and a lot of this will depend on the falconer and also the level of acceptance of the falcon. Without a shadow of a doubt probably the best way to mount a transmitter nowadays is via a Track Pack whereby the transmitter is mounted on the back of the falcon and stays there for the season being switched on and off with a magnetic wand. The transmitter is merely removed once a month or so for battery replacement. Supposedly the batteries will last considerably longer than a month, providing they are switched off after flying each day, but for the sake of just a few pounds each season I prefer to renew them each month. Not all falcons are happy accepting the Track Pack and I tend to think that in these cases they haven't been fitted correctly. Equally true some falcons won't tolerate a tail mounted transmitter. In fact I had an eyass Peregrine Falcon that would destroy a transmitter aerial in seconds' flat if the transmitter was fitted to her tail via a brass tube and a spring clip. But put it on a button bewit around her leg, which you would have thought would be far more likely to cause irritation, and she would totally ignore it. These three methods of attaching transmitters are probably the most commonly used and the safest. Each method has its followers and its detractors but they all have one thing in common. They do not rely on cable ties to be attached to the falcon. Cable tying a transmitter to the anklet is just laziness and shows a lack of pride on the part of the falconer. However this pales into insignificance when compared to those who cable tie a transmitter directly to the leg of the falcon. This is simply outrageous and no person guilty of this crime against falconry can ever even remotely consider themselves a falconer. The possible ramifications of such a negligent action are too horrendous to even contemplate.

For those that do want to mount the transmitter on the tail then the easiest method is to attach a brass tube high up on one of the deck feathers and the transmitter body itself has a spring clip attached. When compressed this spring clip will slide up through the tube and when released open out again holding the transmitter in place. It is virtually impossible for the transmitter to come out of the tube if fitted correctly, not something that is always done when the transmitter is fitted in haste I have to say. The brass tubes are attached to the deck feather with a dab of glue and then crimped with specially made pliers available from the telemetry manufacturers. They are exceedingly expensive in my opinion but they do the job quickly and neatly so I suppose the falconer must grin and bear the expense. Although of course providing they are not lost it is a once only purchase.

There is a very useful little tool called a signal finder on the market that is worth its weight in gold as far as I am concerned as this is a combined magic wand and telemetry transmitter checker. You can switch a magnetic transmitter on and off with the little gadget but you can also check if your transmitter is omitting a healthy signal without having to use the receiver. Very useful if several of you are flying together and at around £35 it is exceedingly good value. Having got used to using one I wouldn't be without it now.

The last item we come to is the glove itself. For Peregrine Falcons I use a single thickness wrist length buckskin glove and have found nothing better over the years. Some would argue that a decent Buckskin glove can be viewed as quite an expensive item. The initial outlay may well seem a little on the expensive side but a decent glove, well looked after and treated with leather dressing when required, will last a very long time and then work out as having cost just a few pounds a year. Buying a cheap glove really is nothing less than a false economy. The falconer needs to be able to feel the jesses of the falcon through the glove, which he is not going to do through some cheap inferior item. A cheap glove very soon becomes hard from blood and chick yolk and it is then virtually impossible to feel the jesses correctly. Once the glove becomes hard it also becomes a difficult surface for the falcon to perch on and she will be uncomfortable when sitting upon it. If nothing else the glove needs to represent a safe and comfortable place for the falcon to be and take her food from. Not a surface that she has to struggle to keep her balance on and one that positively encourages her to want to go elsewhere to perch and or eat. This surely is just about the last thing a falconer should ever wish to induce, his hawk feeling uncomfortable on his glove. It is hard to think of anything that could be greater in terms of negativity. Really that brings us right back to the beginning of the chapter in that you should always buy the best quality equipment you can and treat it well. It pays dividends in the long run. One final thought is, whenever possible purchase your falconry equipment from a supplier that is actually a practising falconer; you would probably be surprised at just how many people that sell falconry furniture are not practising falconers with any real experience under their belts. A sad reflection of the times in which we live.

HOUSING AND WEATHERING

For all my falcons I use a specific type of weathering for housing them on a day to day basis, it is a design that I have honed and fine tuned over my long career as a falconer. I should also state straight away that my hunting falcons live outside in these weatherings in all but the very harshest of weather conditions all year round. So, perhaps I give my weatherings a little more consideration that those falconers that just require such a structure to house their falcon for four or five hours a day. I firmly believe that providing the falcon is protected against the worst of the cold and rain and will not sit in a driving wind, then she is better off breathing fresh air and being out in the light and the elements. It is also my practice with falcons only to use an aviary in the case of moulting or breeding. The only exception to this would be perhaps in the case of a falcon recovering from an accident or long term recuperation from an illness. I have seen falcons that are in flying condition kept in aviaries in the hunting season but other than with social imprints it has to be said that their feather condition clearly reflected the fact. By constantly trying to get to the falconer the wing tips and tail feathers suffer ever increasing amounts of damage, as eventually do the feet and cere. It would be fair, to say I have only ever known of a handful of falcons kept in this manner and their owners seemed oblivious to the damage being done.

When it comes to sighting the weatherings consideration to wind, rain and sun should be taken account of and where possible weatherings built accordingly. Or at least this would be the case in an ideal world. Realistically the falconer may well have to come up and settle upon what amounts to the best compromise possible given the circumstances of his garden layout, family circumstances and neighbours etc. A weathering in recent years has come to mean a safe secure enclosure in which a falcon can sit in and enjoy the fresh air without fear of being molested by a passing dog, fox, cat or wild hawk. Also unfortunately, in our somewhat degenerate times, there is also a case for adding human beings in this list of possible hazard species. The theft of trained hawks are nowhere near as common nowadays as they once were but do still occur occasionally none the less, as regrettably do acts of blatant vandalism and maliciousness. There are still a mindless number that would apparently believe that cutting the leash of a hawk or falcon and letting it take its liberty is a better life for it than that of being tethered to a perch. The fact that the trained hawk gets to fly most days, is well cared for and looked after, both in general husbandry terms and veterinary terms, is neither here nor there. Also the fact that the newly liberated raptor has gone off with its legs shackled together to a somewhat inevitable and lingering end also doesn't seem to occur. Accordingly when it comes to weathering hawks or falcons then, prevention of any possible incident is much better than trying to cope with the aftermath.

My own weatherings are virtually miniature aviaries with either a shelf perch on the back wall or a block perch set in to the ground at one third the overall depth of the weathering from the back wall. The measurements of the weathering I use for a single Peregrine Falcon are six foot high at the front sloping down to five foot six inches at the rear. The width of the weathering is eight feet and the depth is also eight foot. The sides, back and roof are solid sheets of three quarter inch thick board with the roof also covered with heavy duty roofing felt. The side and back boards are covered with feather edging to give a nicer outward appearance and also to give a double skin. The outer side of the boards should receive several coats of weather protection before the feather edge is applied and it goes without saying that the side of the feather edge that will be against the boards will also have received several coats of protection. The front, which has a door set into it, is covered over with one inch by one inch square sixteen gauge wire. The door arrangement also has provision for the fixing of a sturdy padlock. The floor of the weathering is covered with a layer of pea shingle some four inches in depth and this itself sits on a layer of brick rubble and large stones which give the whole arrangement decent drainage. Depending on the position the weathering is erected, it may be advisable to fit a six inch deep board across the width of the weathering at the top to act as a rain guard. This board would also benefit from being covered in roofing felt as it will take the brunt of any driving rain. Should the eventual sighting not be absolutely ideal and additional protection is required from the wind then small conifers such as Leylandii can be planted in the appropriate position to form a natural and not unpleasant looking wind break.

Although I prefer to use pea shingle as a base for both my aviaries and my weatherings I am fully aware that it is far from an ideal material, merely the best, in my opinion, of what is currently available. Personally I much prefer its use however to that of the most readily available alternative which is sand. I find sand becomes clingy when wet and have seen several falcons suffer with abrasions on the feet and legs due to its use. Ideally a fully trained falcon that can be put out to weather should not have a tendency to bate other than on an occasional instance and therefore should not suffer any feather damage as a result of bating on shingle. Despite the protestations of those that prefer sand as a floor material for a weathering I actually find sand is far more abrasive. What on the surface would appear to be a far more creditable objection to the use of pea shingle instead of sand, is the supposed difficulty in obtaining a decent mute sample should one be required. This is very easily overcome by opening up a plastic bin liner and placing it beneath the shelf perch, or if a block is being used instead of shelf perch, merely spike the block through the bin liner and then weight the four corners down with a handful of pea shingle. Very simple and straight forward and because all of the mute will sit on the plastic it is a simple matter to get a decent sample to send to the vet or put under the microscope.

In the use of blocks I have switched for some years now to only those made of plastic with an artificial grass insert in the top. I use six inch diameter blocks for tiercels and eight inch diameter tops for falcons and like mine to raise the feet of the falcon to a point that is a minimum of fifteen inches above the ground. Since switching to plastic blocks for all my falcons I have never ever experienced any foot problems other than those suffered as a result of incidents in the field and one Gyr hybrid male that had bad bumble foot. This was a direct result of his maniacal temper and clutching his own foot in sheer anger and frustration at fumbling his footing and losing his quarry on the ground. The small resultant wounds that he inflicted upon himself, despite being carefully cleansed and treated daily, flared into a nasty case of bumble foot. Unfortunately these wounds required the repeated attention of a vet and a small mortgage to

Haggard Falcon on high block

pay the resultant bill. Since using the plastic type of blocks I am glad to say that it would appear sores and swellings due to inappropriate perching would appear to be a thing of the past. Plastic is also simplicity itself to keep clean, doesn't crack in extreme heat or cold, as wood has a tendency to do, and with a quick wipe with a damp cloth also look smart and presentable.

An item I have become a very staunch fan of, particularly when used with passage falcons, is the high round perch. That is, once the falcon has been manned sufficiently to be able to sit outdoors bareheaded without feeling stressed and thereby causing the falconer untold stress. I like this type of perch because the falcon sits nice and high and they have many of the advantages of the old screen perch without the one major disadvantage that a restless hawk would destroy its tail and wing tips by bating along its length. With the high round perch being the shape it is, this just doesn't happen. Another criticism that used to be levelled against the screen perch is that a sick hawk could not lie down on it and could, in theory, be left sitting upright last thing at night by the falconer only to be discovered hanging dead from the screen in the morning. With the high round perches I use, the circumference is sufficient that even the passage peregrine can lay down if she so requires. My high round perches, which I have specially made, are eight inches in circumference and some forty inches high.

When put out on a lawn to weather then I personally prefer an enclosed area for all the reasons given above with regard to permanent weatherings. Where I live Buzzards and even the occasional Goshawk can present a potential problem. Before anyone scoffs at the thought of a Buzzard killing a Peregrine on the block be aware that I have known of three separate female Goshawks, all in hunting condition, killed at their bows by wild Buzzards as well as one female Goshawk and one Peregrine Falcon killed out in the field by wild Buzzards. The risks are simply too great not to make a safe pen in which to weather hawks an essential item.

The needs of a Peregrine Falcon when it comes to an aviary are no different to any other large falcon. A decent minimum size is an obvious requirement as is providing shelter from the worst of the elements whilst having plenty of perching that will allow the falcon to sit in the sun, particularly so if possible the morning sun. We require that our falcon can enjoy the sun on her plumage if she so desires and also has somewhere to get out of the sun should the temperature prove too much for her. There should be at least a couple of perches that are not covered so as to allow her to enjoy sun and also, just as importantly, the rain when she wants. The perches under cover should allow her protection not only from direct sunlight but also give her complete shelter from north east winds. As we are, I am sure, all more than well aware it is wind chill that can so easily prove fatal to the smaller species of hawks and falcons. Particularly if the instance of possible wind chill occurs when the falcon is already damp. The two elements combine, in so many cases, to become a fatal cocktail. In addition wing tip oedema will also rear its ugly head if careful consideration is not given to the sighting of perches.

The next consideration is should the aviary be an open type, with the majority of the wall construction being of one inch square sixteen gauge wire, or should it be semi seclusion with decent sized windows with appropriate adjacent perches. Bearing in mind we are talking about passage falcons here and not eyasses I personally go for the latter. The falcon has access to visual stimulation as and when she wants it and can get away completely out of sight (in her mind) should she feel threatened. However by the use of carefully selected spy holes and or remote cameras the falconer will always be able to check up on the falcon. The roof will be approximately one third covered over and two thirds open to the elements. As an extra safety precaution the wire roofing material can extend to cover the entire roof included the covered portion, this may well prove useful should the aviary be subjected to a gale at sometime in its life. A wire netting roof can prove troublesome should you have a hawk that has tendency to fly upwards if alarmed. Therefore some people suspend something akin to a large Salmon net around four inches below

Lugger and Lanner Falcons on screen perch

the actual roof. The thought behind this being that there is some give in this netting and it stops the falcon crashing into the harder wire surface at any form of speed. Personally I have never used this type of material as the gauge of the netting tends to mean large squares and I am always concerned a wing or leg could get trapped in it. I have used plastic one inch square netting of the type sold in garden centres for attaching to walls etc to help climbing plants such as Clematis trail themselves up and over a surface. This material still has a small degree of give in it and is relatively cheap and easily obtained.

Life is such, that once again when it comes to sighting the aviary most falconers will probably have to make a compromise with what they have available and sight the aviary accordingly as opposed to what they would ideally prefer. It goes without saying that the aviary in question should be sufficiently large enough and most importantly have plenty of alternative perching sites and surfaces. Do try and make sure though that you avoid the well meaning pitfall of putting a falcon, bearing in mind we are refereeing to a passager not a home produced eyass, in too large an aviary. Try and avoid the aviary being of a sufficient size in any given direction that will enable its resident to build up too much speed and crash into the wire or walls with what could well turn out to be disastrous results. Perches, walls and floors all need to be easily cleanable and for preference I have the floor of all my aviaries covered with pea shingle. I find this material is easy to keep clean with the aid of a power washer and castings dropped on it are easy to spot. The same is true of moulted feathers. Careful thought needs to be given to the placement of a bath so as to enable it to be cleaned and replenished on a regular basis without the need to constantly enter the aviary.

Tiercel on traditional block

As to the perches themselves I use two types in my aviaries when it comes to falcons. Shelf perches with a well known brand of artificial grass inset into them and also bar perches covered in the same grooved rubber material that is to be found on bow perches nowadays or artificial grass. The shelf perches I use are the same size as for a large falcon, which is a half circle with a radius of eight to ten inches or so, depending on manufacturer, and made from plastic. The surface beneath the artificial grass on which the falcon will actually perch has several small holes drilled in it so that these will act as drains with regard to rain water or excess water after cleaning. An important factor to be aware of when buying shelf perches from a falconry equipment manufacturer is the depth of the lip on the outer top edge of the shelf. This lip is designed to keep the artificial grass in place and in theory works very well indeed. However make sure the lip does not exceed the height of the artificial grass when in place or this can lead to the falcon getting sore spots on the feet from the constant rubbing against the plastic. The outer edge of the perch that is at right angles to the flat perching surface is plastic and I always glue a strip of artificial grass on this so as to prevent any possible damage to the rear digit of the falcons' foot. This is a very simple and quick modification to carry out but one that can possibly help to avoid the risk of severe foot problems at a later date.

The bar perches are, in my opinion, a really good idea and are extremely simple to install, keep clean and require no maintenance what so ever.

They basically consist of a metal tube some three inches in diameter and approximately fifteen inches long. This tube has a three inch plate welded one end to close it off and a five inch plate is then welded on the other end at a right angle. This plate has three holes drilled in it in readiness for screwing the perch onto the wall of the aviary. The resulting protruding cylinder is then tightly covered in grooved rubber or artificial grass. The finished article will last a life time and can be quickly and effectively cleaned with a blast or two from a pressure washer.

As with all aviaries I certainly would recommend a double door system or at least a hanging curtain of net on the outside of the entrance door. It has never happened to me but I do know of at least four occasions where both falcons and hawks have been lost because a one door system was used and a resident from an aviary could get across it and out the door a great deal quicker than the falconer concerned had thought possible. It may be an old saying but "better safe than sorry" is an appropriate one never the less.

As mentioned earlier in this chapter, a very important consideration that should never be overlooked is mental stimulation for the falcon when not at work. The view from the aviary should be one that encompasses as much of the surrounding daily life as possible. I like my falcons to be able to see the dogs ambling round the garden and to be able to see people on a daily basis. I don't want that they are shut away in seclusion or isolation and that taking them up from the aviary for flying again at the end of the moult turns into a real trauma for them. However, with the use of an aviary that has closed in sides but with windows for the falcon to look out of it means the falcon, to a large extent, is in control of how much she sees and when. I prefer that my falcons are not allowed to get truly fat when moulting and will still be well enough behaved that I can go into their aviary and take them up onto the fist and put them outside for a while to weather on a block or a high perch. This may well be because I want to give the aviary a clean or carry out some minor maintenance job. Either way I do not want the falcon to become wild and that handling her is as stress free as possible an experience for her.

Having said all of the above with regard to aviaries for moulting etc; I have to be honest and say that in most cases I certainly prefer to moult a falcon at the block for the reasons given in the chapter covering "General Husbandry and Moult".

Peregrines simply love water and bathing and it would be nothing less than cruel not to offer them the opportunity to bath daily through spring, summer and even autumn and at least twice a week during the winter. The only proviso is that the hawk should be fully dry before being put away for the night, especially if they live outside.

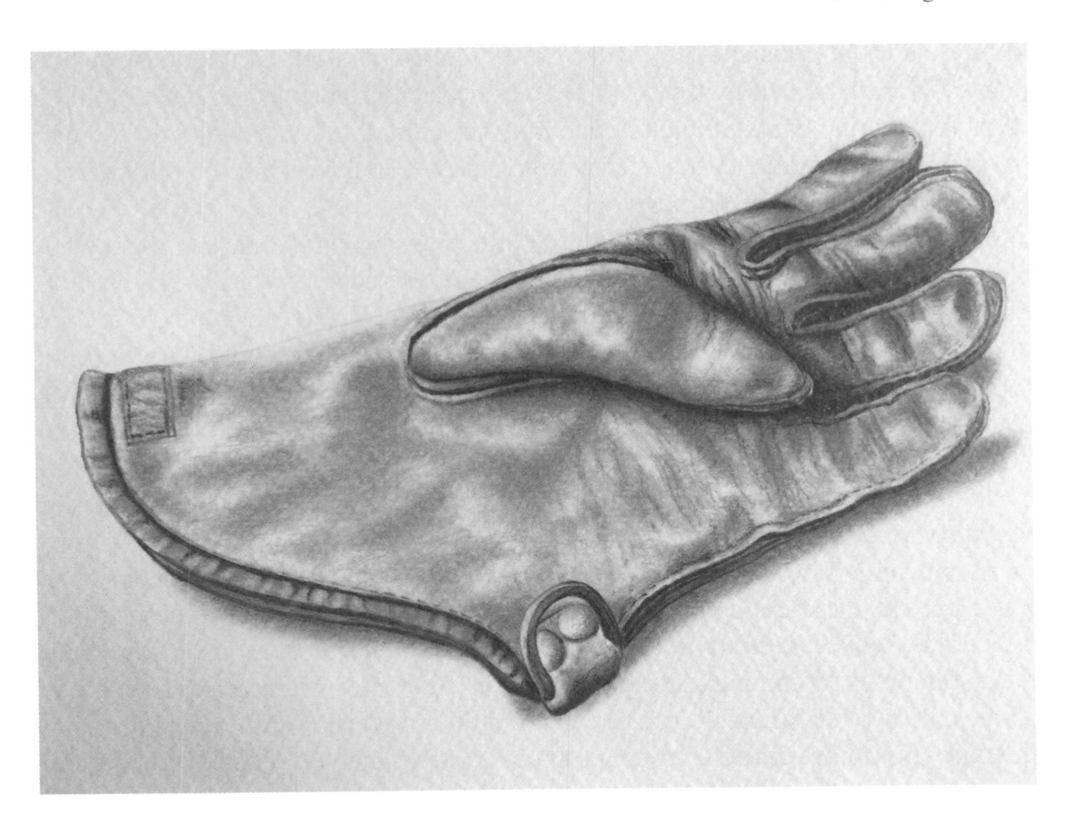

GENERAL HUSBANDRY AND THE MOULT

The day to day home life of a passage falcon will differ very little from that of any other falcon with just a few relatively minor exceptions. As a rule passage falcons, even when intermewed several times, always have a tendency towards restlessness when out on the block weathering. I have experimented with taller blocks on varying heights, by which I mean the falcon sits anything from two to six feet in height above the ground, and have found the results to actually be discouraging. The additional height seems to make the falcon even more restless. It may well be that by raising them up they can then see more places that would be better, in their opinion, to sit and peruse their surroundings. Of course this is, as with practically everything in this book, a personal opinion and not based on any scientific evidence but merely personal observation and even occasionally, hard to believe of me I know, reasoning. As stated in the chapter on equipment I like my blocks around fifteen to twenty inches high so that the falcon is a decent height above the ground as well as the fact her tail is in no danger of being scuffed. I remember a very well known veterinarian giving a talk on perches with regard to weathering and one of the questions he posed his audience was why to we use perches at all? Various ingenious replies were forthcoming from the audience but the plain simple answer was to keep the tail of any hawk or falcon clear of the ground. This was not the only reason but was considered the primary one.

So armed with the knowledge that most passage falcons are somewhat restless when put out on the block to weather, that is when compared to eyasses, then it goes without saying that the sighting of the block is of the utmost importance. Care and attention needs to be paid to what can be seen by the falcon who might strive to get to somewhere she can see that is a more desirable place, in her eyes, to sit. The area chosen needs to be such that the block can be moved around on a regular basis so as to give the ground soiled by the mutes of the falcon a chance to be cleansed either by the elements, or the falconer with a hose or bucket.

A bath needs to be offered on a regular basis and this also needs to be positioned in different spots each day so as to not kill the grass underneath it. When I say on a regular basis, by this I mean in the flying season I offer a bath to the falcon everyday weather permitting; in the winter still at least three times a week. However for a falcon to be offered a bath when weathering I feel that the bath should be removed by around eleven am at the very latest. If the falcon is to be flown that day she will need time to dry off properly, preen and attend to her plumage. Nothing worse than a falcon that suddenly decides it is going to jump into the bath just a short while before the intended leaving time when the bath has been on offer the whole morning. To fly the falcon before she is thoroughly dry or had a chance to attend to her plumage as she desires is a very considerable mistake and my well end in her sitting somewhere to do just that. A thoroughly bad lesson will have been learned by the falcon for the sake of merely taking the bath away well before intended departure time. Again the sizes of baths have been dealt with in the equipment chapter but it should be borne in mind that a decent falconry bath should not need to be filled to the brim. This will effectively prove to be too deep for the falcon and she will have a high degree of hesitancy in stepping in initially. Better three quarters full and she can still dip down and immerse herself completely but doesn't feel at risk entering it.

Out of the flying season then again the bath is still taken away relatively early as the falcon again needs to dry thoroughly before being put away for the night. Also it has to be said I do not offer a bath at all when the weather is damp and foggy or snow is in the air. Straight forward cold weather, providing a North East wind is not blowing, should hold no fear for the falconer and I have known passage peregrines and prairie falcons bathe when the temperature is actually minus. I do need to stress however that the falcon must be thoroughly dry before being put away for the night. If this, for whatever reason, has not been achieved then it is better to bring the falcon in for the night and put her on either a shelf perch or a screen perch.

Let me take this opportunity just to say a few words regarding screen perches and their usage. It has become very much the norm in recent years to decry the screen perch and condemn those that use them as not caring and ignorant when it comes to the welfare of their falcons. Absolutely nothing could in actual fact be further from the truth. There are most certainly occasions when a screen perch is an inappropriate tool and there are equally as many occasions as to when it is an ideal solution to a perching problem. The old arguments levelled against the use of the screen perch don't really hold water when examined closely and, as with nearly everything relating to the general husbandry of falcons, the skill and understanding of the falconer will be the determining factor in when the occasion is the right one or the wrong one. The two most common and oft repeated statements made regarding this type of perch are that a sick falcon cannot lay down on the perch and will therefore hang upside down and probably be found dead in the morning by the falconer. The second is that a restless falcon will bate along the screen perch as opposed to off of it and therefore gradually scrub its train away to a very much shortened mess.

Unless suddenly overtaken by an aneurism, embolism or heart attack a falcon is unlucky as to be so ill that she needs to lay down without the falconer being painfully aware of the fact the falcon is in this condition. Accordingly the falcon will have been removed from the screen perch, or rather refrained from being placed there immediately any deviation in her well being was spotted, and an alternative arrangement made. Such as shelf perch, or indoor block or indeed a travelling box with perch removed can be used as a night quarters temporarily.

As to a falcon scrubbing her tail on the perch by bating along the length of the perch then the remedy is, I am afraid, patently obvious and shouldn't really need explaining. Every action the falcon carries out has a reason behind it. The job and gradually, with experience, the skill of the falconer is to interpret these actions and the reasons behind them and effect a remedy either through straight forward application of a change in circumstance or taking training in a certain area a little deeper perhaps. The sighting of the screen perch may be making the falcon restless because there is a much more desirable place to sit right in her eye line and to her it seems such a much more attractive proposition that she constantly tries to get there. Remedy is simple, move the sight of the perch or move, what patently to her is the more desirable one. As to the tail scrubbing again either the perch is sighted in the wrong place and the falcon is trying to

Intermewed Falcon enjoying bath

make her way along the perch to what she considers a superior place to spend her time or she is somewhat lacking in her manning and taming. Again remedy is patently obvious, or should be, and effecting a cure straight forward enough.

Not really an example to draw a direct comparison from, but I do know of a small falconry centre where three falcons were in residence and despite having nicely constructed weatherings were in fact very restless on their blocks. A shed type building with an open front was constructed looking out towards open fields and a hill and then a screen perch fitted the length of it going across the shed. This was so any falcon sitting on the screen perch looked out over the pastoral vista. The transformation was amazing and all three falcons instantly relaxed and the owner of the centre thinks this is the best thing he has ever done. Let me hasten to add, the falcons are put away at night in a hawk house on shelf perches and not left to the mercies of predators, both two and four legged, that patrol the fields at night.

A falcon needs to be fed a variety of food items to keep her at her best and with modern food suppliers that specialise in raptor food so very easily located on the internet obtaining the same should not present a problem. Nowadays chicks, quail, rats, mice, rabbits and various other food items are generally speaking readily available and certainly do not cost a fortune. Stocking a freezer with a wide selection is still remarkably cheap. One plea I will make and I know that it is still unfortunately a very relevant one, is do not feed road kill under any circumstances. I have heard so many horror stories over the years and have known of one falcon that died as a result of being fed road kill and another that was ill for a considerable time. There are those, which despite the obvious pit falls of feeding such food, still continue to do so with the mantra that nothing bad has ever happened. This may well be true up to that point but it only takes one bad experience to be the fatal one and there will be no going back from it.

An argument often put forward by those that insist on feeding such food is that they only feed road kill that they have seen killed or have hit with their car themselves. The thinking behind this is that the kill is obviously fresh and the fact it was moving sufficiently to be hit means it must be okay. I find this a simply ludicrous form of logic. Does it not occur to anyone that perhaps the victim was hit because it was unwell and as such its reactions were not what they should have been? Why take a risk on such an unreliable and unknown food source, particularly as when previously stated hawk food from a commercial supplier is still so cheap in relative terms. At the time of writing I worked out that feeding a passage falcon good high quality food and without feeding her any of her kills would still only amount to around ninety five pounds a year. Would anyone really want to potentially risk the health of their falcon for such a minimal amount, if they would then perhaps they are involved in the wrong sport.

The question of vitamins and dietary supplements is one I have rather mixed feelings about if I am completely honest. I have a tendency every now and then to think I will use them on a regular basis and buy the stock in and plan out a dietary regime including their usage and make a start. I am almost ashamed to say that after a week or two the new regime has normally fallen by the wayside and we go back to just relying on good quality food as is the norm. I realise in the case of those that breed falcons the question of vitamins and supplements is a totally different one and an egg laying female would no doubt benefit greatly from the presumed beneficial addition to her diet. In my own case my rather pathetic excuse for the hit and miss approach is that I have other falcons that are used for bird control and display work to look after and accordingly the specialised diet plan tends to fall by the wayside quite easily.

The moult is a time of year, particularly if I am fortunate enough to be in the process of intermewing a passage falcon, where I do make an effort with additional vitamins and calcium and do my very best to stick to any formulated plan relating to diet.

It goes without saying that different foods have the potential to offer different protein levels and also vary in the richness or otherwise of particular vitamins. As a base diet most falconers nowadays use day old cockerels which are freely available, exceedingly cheap when purchased in even relative modest amounts and are useful in being quite uniform and a known quantity when it comes to protein and size. Rabbit is a useful occasional change for a Peregrine but is a light meat and not containing a great deal of protein. It is a useful food when going through the process of bringing down the condition of a falcon. Full crops can be fed and still the condition of the falcon will gradually lower. The emphasis here being very much on the gradually. I would not feed rabbit to a falcon for more than two consecutive days because there are alternatives that will achieve the same end without the need for constant repetition of a particular food. For example day old chicks with all their innards popped out, washed meat are equally good at reducing the condition of a falcon. Although I do not use washed meat myself as is explained later in this chapter. Some people feed day old Turkey chicks as these are considerably larger than Cockerel chicks. My personal experience with them is that I don't like using them and found them messy to use and they didn't seem to be as high in protein as cockerel chicks. This is purely my opinion and I may well be wrong but I was happier not feeding them and accordingly do not feel I should heartily recommend them to others.

Game birds, Quail, Grouse, Partridge and Pheasant are all good high protein foods but ensure the strips of yellow fat on Pheasant are removed before feeding. Ducks are good quality food but tend to be very fatty. Rooks and other Corvids are good red meat and high in protein but some falcons have a great tendency to dislike the taste (even successful rook hawks) and it has to be said that lice can be a very great problem with them and care should be taken if they are fed on a regular basis. Pigeons of all descriptions, including Woodpigeons, are a favourite of falcons and are without doubt good nourishing food. They do however bump the weight and condition of a falcon up very quickly and should be fed sparingly. Old pigeons tend to be tough and indigestible so feed with caution if at all. Moorhens and Coots have a tendency to be very fat and greasy and personally I never fed to falcons at all.

Rats, those produced domestically, are a very good source of food and falcons thrive on them and I endeavour to feed them to my falcons at least once a week. They are however lacking in Carotene and if fed too often the falcon will maintain condition but her cere and feet will lose their natural yellow colouring and turn almost white which really does look awful, especially on a passage falcon that arrived with such a depth of colour. The key to good health in the falcon is a balanced and varied diet just as it is with a human being. Undoubtedly a falcon could survive on a diet of nothing but day old chicks interspersed occasionally with the odd kill she has achieved, but surely no falconer would want to subject his falcon to this. If the falcon depicts an image of health and happiness then this reflects in a positive manner on the falconer. Also don't forget what Symon Latham, who from his writings appeared to understand the needs of maintaining a passage falcon in the most robust of health, had to say in 1615 "Wash'd meat and stones maketh a hawk to flie, but great casting and long fasting maketh her to die"

The moult is a process the falcon and the falconer have to go through each year. This may seem an odd thing to say that the falconer also goes through the moult but he or she will have made preparations and probably a plan of action and will need to implement and maintain it through the five to seven month process. The moult, which normally begins in late March or early April, is a critical time for the falcon and she needs to be thoroughly relaxed and have good high quality food to see her body through the enormously complicated and no doubt draining process. The sequence in which a falcon changes her feathers is far from random and in all but the very occasional odd ball case, follows a well documented order. In the case of the wings it is the seventh primary or beam feather and the corresponding secondary feather that will drop first. When the replacements for these are almost down then the next pair will drop and so on accordingly. The falcon will moult from the centre of the wings outwards with the last wing feathers to be replaced being the first or very outer primaries.

My Haggard Falcon Grace

The train or tail is moulted concurrently and the centre deck feathers are the first to drop, normally within a few hours of each other. When the new decks are almost down then the next pair will drop and so on. Again the moulted feathers are dropped in pairs from the centre of the train outwards with the very outside pair being the last to drop. Body feathers tend to drop once the moulting of the main flight feathers is well under way. Every falconer has his or her preference for how the moult is approached and seen through. Some put the falcon concerned into an aviary and literally pile in the food, which will be of the highest quality, in the hopes of getting good strong growth and the moult completed as quickly as possible. Others use a system of controlled artificial daylight in attempts to hasten the moult. Personally I tend to think that nature knows best and let the moult take place at the speed that falcon is happy with. I don't play with artificial daylight, don't give vitamin injections, and I certainly don't give weird and wonderful combinations of vitamins and animal glands. I feed good quality food, very slightly more than normal, however I do not massively change the routine of the falcon, other than in the fact she is not flying daily. I much prefer to moult my falcons in what is referred to as "on the fist" style. That is the falcon is put out to weather daily having been hooded and weighed as normal then left to weather, normally with a decent tiring to keep her occupied. Later in the day she is taken up on the fist, carried for a while, and then fed on the fist. When she has finished her meal and been allowed to clean her toes, search the glove for any missed morsel and finally feaked on the glove she is hooded up and carried to her weathering, unhooded, and put away for the night.

For me the great advantage of this system, although a little time consuming, is that the falcon remains manned, happy in the presence of the falconer and still looks forward to the daily contact even though hers is probably only food motivated and not involving any degree of affection as is no doubt felt towards her by the falconer. Really this period can be used so much to the advantage of the falconer. With the judicious use of tirings, meals and general on the fist time can be extended to be any duration the falconer sees fit. The manning and taming process continues, which can only be advantageous to both parties, but the reclaiming process will be one of almost inconsequential passing. No trauma to be endured by either party as wildness and bad manners on the part of the falcon have not been allowed to enter into the equation. All that is required at the end of the moult is a little judicial feeding and the use perhaps of rangle, rabbit and washed meat to remove surplus fat and then the process of getting the falcon back into condition, both mentally and physically, can gently take place. A stress free transition from not working and moulting to flying and getting fit again ready to hunt for a living once more.

It is, unfortunately, not an exaggeration to say I do know of a number of falcons that have been ruined when being brought out of the moult, particularly when they have been moulted out loose in an aviary. There seems to be a school of thought in certain quarters that to reduce the weight fairly quickly and get the falcon on the wing and supposedly muscling up as fast as possible is the way to go. In my opinion nothing could be further from the truth. Particularly in the case of the intermewed passage falcon that was flown in her fist season. Her fitness never truly totally disappears and getting her back on the wing doesn't have to be rushed and there is no yardstick by which any one falcon can be measured as to what the specific speed of its progress should be when being reclaimed and got fit for hunting again. Obviously it should not take an inordinately long time but the old saying regarding "making haste slowly" is never truer than when working with falcons. Hal Webster always used to say he guided falcons he didn't train them. Personally I feel this is a very apt way of putting things.

No falconer ever attempts to bludgeon or coerce a falcon into doing what is required by them. Nor should the desired result in the falcon be brought about by starving the falcon into submission. This latter course of action will very swiftly be repaid by either a lost falcon or one whose health deteriorates very quickly indeed. Either way the so called falconer should be thoroughly ashamed of themselves and their lack of understanding of what is really required. A thin falcon too often denotes she has been trained by starvation rather than by skill and understanding of her needs and ways. Just as "a fat hawk makes a lean horse, a weary falconer and an empty purse" a falcon that is too thin will lose her strength and flying prowess and though this lack of power she will appear to lose her courage by constantly refusing quarry.

When taking a falcon up from the moult, no matter by which method she has undergone her yearly change, treat her almost as if taken on the fist for the very first time and be extremely methodical in your approach to her conditioning and over all reclaiming. Reduce her body fat and then if necessary her body mass gradually and use plenty of tirings during the process. Do not let the falcon get bored with sitting on your fist or being in your company. For the falconer the pleasure of the falcon on the fist is reward in itself but the same is not true of the falcon. If she has been manned and tamed as she should, she will not find being with the falconer an unpleasant experience but the falconer should want to promote more than that in his charge. The fact that it is through the stomach of the falcon that the falconer wins tolerance and then the confidence of the falcon is hardly a great secret. Accordingly make sure the freezer has a good stock of varied tirings in it so that when on the fist the falcon can be, from her point of view, pleasurably occupied. It never ceases to amaze me how few falconers use tirings nowadays and in fact how many there are that do not even know what tirings are.

Finally it should also be borne in mind passage falcons are very erratic moulters at least in their first change of plumage and quite often it can take two or even three moults before every last trace of brown has disappeared completely. My own personal opinion is that the better manned and truly tamed the passager is the better she will moult. It makes sense that a falcon who is content with her life, albeit that she is sharing it with a human, is getting plenty of good quality food without being over exerted at any point is more likely to give in the wishes of her body and change her plumage. Also she will have sufficient vitamins etc in her daily food to ensure the new growth should be strong and healthy. Despite the fact it happens every year the moult really is a major process that a falcon has to go through and anything the falconer can do to ease the transition in plumage has to be a very good thing.

For those unfamiliar with the terms I have used in this chapter I will take a few lines to explain them. “Rangle” are small rounded pea sized stones that can be given orally to a falcon after her meal, which will not have contained casting material. The idea is the stones will break up the accumulated fat and grease in the crop and panel and then be regurgitated in the morning as would a normal casting. After two or three times of rangle being administered it will be noticed that the mutes of the falcon are discoloured and probably foul smelling. This is merely the fat being expelled and should not cause undue concern on the part of the falconer. After each cast the stones can be collected up, washed and held in readiness for another application. Many falcons will pick rangle for themselves; I have noticed this is especially true after having enjoyed a bath. The stones can also be given by hiding in a morsel of food that is large enough to hide the stone but small enough to be swallowed whole quite comfortably.

Washed meat is quite simply what it says it is. It consists of strips of perfectly lean beef that have been soaked in cold water for several hours and then dried thoroughly on a cloth or paper towel, not dried by means of artificial heat being applied. This is then fed to the falcon and acts as a mild purgative and obviously contains no goodness or protein what so ever. This will not be palatable to the falcon and so I would advise not feeding it to her on your fist. Either get someone else to do it, so as she doesn’t associate the meal with you, or feed her at perch. This is the one time I would recommend not feeding the falcon on the glove as a matter of course. Are falcons sufficiently intelligent that getting someone else to feed them on the fist removes the thought from their mind that you were responsible for this poor quality meal? I very much believe so and would act accordingly if I was to feed washed meat. However I have to be truthful and say I used washed meat once, many years ago, on a particularly difficult haggard Lugger Falcon in the hopes of sharpening her appetite. The after affect of the washed meat was that she was certainly off colour for a while and dropped condition quite rapidly. It took several days of high quality food, given in generous portions, to get us back to where we had been before the start of the exercise. So washed meat for me is not ever part of my weight reduction plan.

Tirings are a food item designed to give the falcon very little reward for a great deal of time consuming expended effort. Chicken necks, pigeon wings with most of the meat taken off, front leg of rabbit with most of the meat removed and other similar bony, sinewy items. The falcon pulls and pulls at them because she can clearly see food on them but the effort and concentration required to win each small morsel takes time and so the falconer can prolong the meal far past what it would normally take the falcon to consume her daily rations. For me tirings are an indispensible training and taming aid. There are others of much greater stature who have obviously felt the same way and I make no excuse for quoting Turberville from 1575 "I have knowne many Falconers that never make their hawkes to tyre, saying that it is but a custom, and needelesse; but I say contrary, for in as much as the hawke is exercised by reasonable tyring she becometh the healthier and the lighter both of body and of head by all the moderate exercise, yea, and she is the better in state also as you may perceive".

Chicken and Duck necks are now readily available from the larger hawk food suppliers and therefore it presents no problem in having a decent stock of them. If I were, for some reason or another, to be reduced to using one type of tiring only however, then it would undoubtedly be the front leg of the humble rabbit. For what I want to use them for they are quite simply perfect.

THE PASSAGE FALCON

"But leaving to speak any more of these scratching kinde of hawks, that I never did love should come too neare my fingers and to return to the courteous and faire conditioned haggard faulcon, whose gallant disposition, I know not how to extol or praise so sufficiently as she deserves". Simon Latham 1615.

Just what is it about the Passage Falcon that quickens the blood of any true falconer and fires a deep passion that seems to grow in intensity with the passing of the years? For someone that has never had the privilege of flying one then it may well be difficult to understand the depth of admiration they provoke in an experienced falconer. Gilbert Blaine, surely one of the most gifted and respected falconers of all time, in his book simply entitled "Falconry", started his chapter on passage falcons with a quote taken from Gerald Lascelles in his book "The Art of Falconry" written in 1892. In such vaulted company I make no excuse or apology for doing the same. *"What the professional is to the amateur, or rather, perhaps, what the thorough bred horse is to all other varieties of the equine race, the passage hawk is, according to species, to every other hawk that is trained, in as much as she is swifter, more active, and more powerful than the nestling".*

The very obvious advantages of training and flying a passage falcon as opposed to an eyass is that the falcon will have already fended and hunted for herself for several months now and the very fact that she has come into your hands proves she is successful at what she does and not one of the very high percentage of youngsters that would fall by the wayside in the process of natural selection. With the vast majority of falcons, especially those flown in the Western world, being eyass falcons that have been produced in aviaries in a domestic situation I personally feel the modern falconer is not really in a position to judge just how big the gap in performance in the field can be. If you stop and think about things logically, the performance capabilities between an eyass and a passager simply cannot be on a par in all but a very few exceptional cases. This is certainly at least for the first one or two seasons anyway whilst the eyass slowly learns all that the passager had to learn very quickly, or if not, then perish. It is true that hunger is a very significant spur to the learning curve of a young falcon, or in fact any predator, winged or otherwise. I always have a little inward smile to myself when very prominent display givers expound about there being no difference what so ever between the captive bred and wild peregrine falcon in terms of capability. With an eyass this may well be true as the falconer is the only instructor from the time the falcon first starts to fly. However with the passager the parents, as well as nature itself, have honed her skills and done so very effectively otherwise she simply would not have survived.

With domestic production of raptors for falconers there are such a large number of variables that will have an effect on the eyass that the falconer eventually receives. Despite the fact that it is glaringly obvious that only the finest of hunting falcons, both potential parents having been proved repeatedly in the field should be paired up, this rarely happens. How often have I heard the phrase "this falcon isn't very good so I will stick her in for breeding". This is exactly the sort of falcon you should not be wanting as the basis of your breeding stock. However realistically how many falconers consign their very best hunting falcons to the breeding chamber, especially those that take on out of the hood flights as it means they will miss a large chunk of their season to do so. Also the risk of a pair not settling together peacefully will weigh heavily on the mind. When you have a falcon or a tiercel that is a jewel above and beyond what you have flown before, it is difficult to take a conscious decision to stop flying them and pair them up in a breeding project.

Then there is the survival rate. In the wild the passage falcon that comes into the hands of the fortunate falconer may well be the only survivor from the clutch of which she was a part. All of the eggs in the clutch may not have hatched; siblings may or may not have reached fledgling stage and also may or may not have reached the stage where they set off on passage. Nature is a hard and exacting master and mistakes and the general inexperience of the young falcon are quite often punished very severely. It is an accepted and somewhat shocking fact that mortality rates amongst young peregrines can be as high as seventy per cent in the first six months of life. In the case of the aviary produced eyass the mortality rate is exceptionally and artificially low. With advancements in incubation and hatching techniques, as well as the relative equipment, a very high percentage of fertile eggs are now hatched successfully. With striding advances in veterinary medicine it also means that eyass survival rate is very many times higher than in the wild. Complications such as yolk sacs that have failed to retract or are indeed infected, which in the wild will mean the inevitable death of the chick, are treatable with a high survival rate when it comes to captive bred eyasses. Accordingly many falcons that would have been weeded out by nature make it to point in their lives where they can be taken up for training. Does that automatically mean that because these young falcons have progressed this far that they have the where with all to make good hunting falcons?

Stuffed Falcon, supposedly Sultan, on screen perch at Valkenswaard

I can only illustrate the point I am trying to make by, somewhat laboriously no doubt, recalling two hawks that came into my falconry life. A very good number of years back now I had a captive bred male Red Naped Shaheen. He was the only egg in the clutch that hatched and he went on to be parent raised before I collected him. On the day of collection I helped the breeder catch him up out of the aviary, fit his falconry furniture there and then, and he then sat on the fist for the long drive home. So training literally commenced right away. This male Shaheen flew at one pound, one and a quarter ounces (490 grams) and killed Partridge, Rook, various small birds before being given a serious chance at Red Grouse. People literally laughed when I said I was taking this small falcon, along with two Peregrine Falcons, with me grouse hawking in Scotland. Not only did he kill grouse and kill them in style but he is the only falcon I have ever had kill two out of the same covey on the same flush. He cut one down in the stoop and then threw up, stooped again, and bound to another. I was so in awe of his temperament, his willingness to fly any quarry and his tenacity when doing so that I ordered a falcon from the same pairing for the following season.

On collecting my new falcon the following year the clutch had consisted of four eggs, three had hatched and there were two females and a male. I chose the female I wanted, again went in with the breeder and caught her up and fitted her falconry furniture. Just as with the male the previous year she was hooded up and taken home on the fist and her subsequent training matched that of her sibling from the previous year in every respect. However this falcon turned out to have no fire, no enthusiasm and never caught quarry. In fact I would think she would struggle to catch a cold. I eventually gave her to a friend that did display and clearance work and he flew her for a number of years but in his view she was lazy and would do as little as possible to get her food. In my opinion this falcon in the wild would have been one of the seventy per cent that just doesn't make it.

To the falconer with an eye to appreciate such things the passager will always stand out as being such even if she has been intermewed several times in captivity. The fact that she has moulted and shed her juvenile plumage in exchange for that of an adult does nothing to change the stance, the way in which the head and particularly her shoulders are held and the special look in her eye. Now this may well sound like being a little farfetched or trying to ascribe to myself skills that are simply not there. However I will illustrate the point by recollecting a visit to the annual Sky trials held in Ejica, Southern Spain, a good number of years ago. I was standing close to the weathering area admiring the falcons, some forty plus in number, sitting there quietly on their blocks. Approximately half were Peregrine Falcons, some in immature plumage but the majority were intermewed falcons. A German falconer wandered over and we got into conversation and he asked which falcon I most like the look of. I pointed out a falcon that was intermewed and said she was the best looking falcon for me and was obviously taken as a passager. He expressed the opinion that she too was the pick for him and he also thought she was a passage falcon that had been intermewed. We eventually found out who owned the falcon and it turned out it was indeed a four times intermewed passager. She carried herself differently enough for the experienced eye to still be able to distinguish the traits that made her that little bit different.

At another Sky Trials event at Ejica a few years later I also had an exceedingly effective demonstration of the difference in flying style between a captive bred eyass falcon and a passager both still in their first seasons. As readers will be aware a Sky Trial is basically a competition to see whose falcon performs best on the day in the opinion of a panel of judges, made up of falconers. The method employed to ensure the falcons fly hard and with serious intent is to throw out a strong racing pigeon. In this way there is a constant, applied to all falcons entered, whereby position, stoop, tenacity etc can be effectively compared between falcons. The falcons being entered to the trials will have been flying pigeons in the same manner for a considerable time before the event and therefore know what is happening and the importance of pitch and position in relation to the falconer. So these dimensions, that are rate of climb and positioning, are also judged and awarded points on a pre-determined scale.

The falconer walks out into the middle of a cleared area and when he is happy with the height and position of his falcon signals an assistant, who has been chosen at random by the judges, to throw out a pigeon that has been selected by an independent person. The stoop, kill, or throw up and chase are all judged and marked accordingly. On the occasion in question a particularly beautiful eyass falcon of the year was being flown and, according to those who had seen her fly before, was apparently well worth watching. When the falcon left the fist she mounted very quickly indeed and positioned herself over the falconer, certainly it became obvious in a matter of minutes that she really did know what was expected and how to deal with it. When the falconer was happy the signal was given and the pigeon thrown out. There was very little wind at all but the pigeon was thrown directly into what little there was. As soon as the falcon saw the pigeon released from the hand it turned over and started to stoop. Being aware of the falcon the pigeon turned downwind and was very narrowly missed by the falcon on the initial stoop but was indeed taken after the falcon had thrown up and then put in a short stoop and came up to the pigeon from behind and slightly underneath and bound to it. A good flight from a falcon that knew what was happening and how to deal with it and accordingly was marked very highly by the judges.

Next up was the passage falcon and the same initial scenario unfolded. The falconer walked in the cleared area, unhooded the falcon, and she wasted very little time in leaving the fist and starting to climb very rapidly indeed. The falcon was soon showing she was ready by sitting on her wings, however unlike the eyass who had been more or less directly overhead, the passage falcon waited on slightly to one side and just a little behind the falconer. When the pigeon was thrown out, again directly into what little wind there was, it made off in a straight line as the falcon was behind it and not directly over it. The falcon powered forward and continued to rise as she did so. After approximately eighty to a hundred yards the pigeon obviously began to feel very intimidated and turned back downwind. Only then did the passage falcon stoop and at the end of it she hit the pigeon very hard and as it tumbled earthwards she threw up and over and bound to it before it had fallen very far. A magnificent demonstration of tactics as well as flying prowess. The flight itself raised a very generous round of applause from the falconers gathered to watch the trials.

As to the ethics of Sky Trials themselves that is a question that I prefer not to get into in this book. Suffice it to say I have never participated in them as a falconer nor have I ever used any live pigeons or bagged game when it comes to training falcons. I personally don't believe in it and like to think I can train a falcon effectively without recall to their use. That doesn't necessarily mean I decry those that do or in fact Sky Trials themselves. I have actually been a judge on a couple of occasions where Sky trials are perfectly legal and considered a matter of course by those that participate in them. This was in South Africa and Mexico. At both these events the winners were falcons that were hunted at ducks on a daily basis. Therefore they understood perfectly about positioning and height and, from their point of view, merely hunted a pigeon instead of a duck.

The passage falcon has been used, with considerable success it must be said, for waiting on flights, especially at Red Grouse on the moors of Northern England and Scotland. Waiting on flights were formerly considered more suited to the eyas falcon and it was thought that a passage falcon would all too easily take any given opportunity to fly at check and accordingly be unsuitable for the flight. It was originally the Dutch school of falconry that gradually brought about a change in this thinking and passage falcons were flown at game in the waiting on style. However generally speaking, certainly in Great Britain, the eyas still remained the norm and made up the vast majority of falcons flown at Grouse, Partridge and Pheasant each season. It was falconers that were acknowledged by their peers as being outstanding in their field that gradually brought about an acceptance and indeed a desire for passage falcons to take their rightful place on the cadge. Falconers such as Geoffrey Pollard whose cadge at one time was made up exclusively of passage falcons for his annual treks north each year. One of the most famous hawks of relatively modern times was in fact a passage falcon "The Pro" flown by him at grouse for a number of years, but more of her later.

However it was principally for out of the hood flights that the passager was formerly so highly prized and considered de rigour. Flights such as those against Kites and Herons a cast of passage falcons would be considered the right tool for the job. When both of these quarries became, to all intents and purposes, unavailable the Rook superseded them as a somewhat poorer but still enjoyable replacement. For the Rook, one passage falcon would be flown on its own unless being flown as perhaps a make hawk for another falcon. For the flight at Kites then, passage Gyrs would also be used and probably the most famous depiction there is of Kite Hawking shows a cast of Gyrs taking a Kite. This renowned picture was painted by Joseph Wolf in 1856 and shows a white and a grey Gyr coming to terms with an unfortunate Red Kite.

When Kite Hawking, from a combination of reasons, became almost impossible to engage in properly and a sufficiently regular basis to warrant keeping one or two casts of falcons purely for this flight, an alternative had to found. The Heron was deemed to be the appropriate alternative as, at the time, it could be found in sufficient numbers in the right sort of open countryside and was a testing flight for a cast of falcons. Passage peregrines and indeed initially passage Gyrs were flown at Herons but the Gyrs were found to be an overmatch for the Heron and when they could be induced to fly them would almost inevitably either kill or cripple their quarry. The falconers of the day did not want to unnecessarily kill the Herons and much preferred to ride up quickly to falcons and their prize and if at all possible take them up from the Heron. Having been checked over, if the Heron was found to be fine it would be released to perhaps provide a flight another day or off spring that would do the same.

Heron Hawking was taken to dizzy heights between 1839 and 1855 with the establishment and subsequent operations of The Loo Hawking Club. This was a Dutch Anglo enterprise that had the blessing of King William the third of Holland and enjoyed Royal Patronage from both Crown Prince Alexander and Princess Sophie. English falconer Edward Clough Newcombe was secretary and very much the driving force behind the club. Whilst Newcombe was secretary of The Loo Club the arrangement was that Dutch falconers would provide twenty two falcons for the chase and their English counterparts the same number. Herons were abundant and obtaining flights on passage, so as to have the right ingredients for the "Haut Vol" or ringing flight, were in place. The Loo Club did try a very small number of Gyrs at Herons but it was the passage peregrine that was considered the perfect falcon for this particular flight. In the relatively short life of this highly prestigious club somewhere in the order of twenty-three hundred Herons were taken by the falcons and it has to be said that the vast majority were released again unharmed. A Heron had a ring fitted to its leg before being released and there is record of one particular Heron being caught on no less than nine separate occasions.

Newcombe, on the eventual demise of The Loo Hawking Club, carried on hawking herons in Norfolk as best he could and in 1863 was amongst the small band of dedicated falconers that formed the Old Hawking Club. With Heron Hawking in England not really a viable sporting proposition again an alternative quarry had to found and this was the slightly more humble but still exceedingly sporting Rook. This is the principal quarry the Old Hawking Club pursued with vigour until its eventual demise in 1926. Although Game birds, Magpie and Lark also featured on the quarry lists it was out of the hood flights with passage falcons that was the mainstay of the club's sporting activities.

For those that still have doubts that you can stoop a falcon to the lure, fly it out of the hood at quarry and then switch it to waiting on flights for game let me relate the standard practice of the OHC when dealing with passage falcons. Each season the club would draft in eight to ten fresh passage falcons that had been trapped by the Mollen family in Valkenswaard. These would be to replace those lost, killed and sold off to members of the club. These fresh falcons would be trained for the flight at rook and then switched to waiting on flights for Grouse. Only the very exceptional and the very finest performers against rook would be held back for the following season, to once again be flown at the sable quarry.

Passage falcons that have written their own names in the annals of history through their exploits and endeavours are many and picking just a few out to illustrate how good some of them were has been difficult. However in my own mind, and anything like this has to come from personal feelings, there are several falcons from history that seem to stand out just that little bit higher than others. Without a moment's hesitation the first two of these that I would choose would be "Sultan" and "De Ruyter" falcons that were taken on passage in 1842. They were owned by Edward Clough Newcombe and trained by his falconer John Pells, the English born son of famous Dutch professional falconer Jan Pells. Flown at herons as part of the hawking stud of The Loo Hawking Club, this cast did particularly well and in the season of eighteen forty three took fifty-four herons and the following season took a further fifty-seven. Unfortunately "De Ruyter" was lost later in the same season when being flown in a cast with another falcon at rooks on Lakenheath Warren in Suffolk. Both falcons chased a rook downwind never to be seen again.

The following season "Sultan" took three herons on her own and also twenty-five rooks. Her portrait, executed by none other than Sonderland, is a

Passage Falcon

very famous iconic falconry image. In the Culture museum in Valkenswaard, Holland there is a large and fascinating exhibition devoted to falconry as it featured in the life of the town and on a screen perch with various falcons upon it is a stuffed falcon which visitors are assured is "Sultan". I don't know whether it is or not but certainly it is nice to think that she is still with us in one form or another.

A passage falcon of 1875 that also wrote her own place in falconry history was "Bois de Luc", named after the small town close to where she was taken. Trapped by Mollen and sent over for the Old Hawking Club she was originally trained in the North of England and came south for the spring rook hawking season of 1866 with high expectations of her abilities. At first she disappointed members of the club with simply refusing to fly rooks at all. The club persisted with her and she killed a couple of easy rooks and still continued to refuse more than she took on. Eventually she flew and caught a good strong rook and from then on flew them with gusto. In fact of the next sixty slips she was given at rooks she only missed one.

"Bois de Luc" continued to be a very successful rook hawk for the next four seasons and was eventually lost for three weeks in the October of 1880. Once safely recovered she was given to a falconer in Cornwall, who flew her at rooks but kept her at semi hack. Unfortunately the life of this falcon was taken when she was shot on a rook in the March of the following year.

"The Duck-Killer" is a passage falcon that many more falconers already know more about than they actually realise. A great number of falconers that are interested in the history of the sport are familiar with the story of the time Adriaan Mollen was trapping the passage falcons in 1872 and as he took a falcon out of the bow net a particularly large dark falcon appeared and saw Mollen. She flew off but was back before too long. However having been spooked by seeing Mollen she would put in half hearted stoops at the lure pigeons but she would not commit herself to a full attack and worse still, from Mollen's point of view, she would not allow any other falcon to linger long enough to take the hawk catchers bait. This beautiful dark falcon was there day after day but would not come in herself and made sure that no other falcon would come in either.

With his season passing him by Mollen began to despair and eventually took his gun with him intending to shoot the falcon should she appear. The falcon failed to appear and was not seen in that immediate vicinity again and so Adriaan Mollen, no doubt relieved, went back to his trapping. One of his sons had been working a trapping hut many miles away and a week later came home with his prize, a beautiful dark falcon that the older man instantly recognised. It was the falcon that had caused him so much trouble and frustratingly had caused a number of other passage falcons to pass on by.

The falcon was sent over for The Old Hawking Club and was apparently blessed with a particularly fine temperament. She was also an excellent hunting falcon and killed more than forty rooks in her first season. She was eventually lost flying rooks in Norfolk.

"Danceaway" has to be another passage falcon that has earned its place in the falconry hall of respect. Taken on passage in 1892 she was entered to rooks in the spring of the following year. Her career as a rook hawk did not get off to a very promising start with and she was apparently considered something of a clumsy footer in her early days. However she appears to have learnt with experience though and ended her first season with sixty rooks to her foot. She continued to fly well for the next five seasons taking a further two hundred and sixteen rooks but had taken to ignoring the lure after an unsuccessful flight and flying at check at other rooks. Most of the time she would be recovered quickly as the resultant kill from flying at check was still in sight. But on occasion she was left out and when taken up again a few days later would be as good mannered as when she left.

In the season of 1899 she strayed and stayed out once too often. Chasing what would have been her thirteenth rook of the season she met with her death due to an ignorant soul with a gun.

There have been many successful passage falcons since the heady days of The Old Hawking Club and again there are those that stand just that little bit taller than the rest. Surely one of this has simply got to be "The Pro".

Originally taken in Pakistan in 1960 and sent over to England that winter, this falcon was a gift for Michael Woodford. Mike wasn't in a position at the time to fly the falcon and so it was loaned to Geoffrey Pollard for the 1961 season. In her first season at Red Grouse she managed a respectable tally of fourteen and was duly returned to Mike.

For the season of 1962 Mike loaned her again to Geoffrey and she improved dramatically as a game hawk and her score rose to twenty-one Grouse. It was during this season that Mike gave the falcon to Geoffrey on a permanent basis and the famous partnership, which was to last for a further four years and eventually account for a total of one hundred and forty-one Red Grouse, moved forward. In the season of 1968 she was left out one night, bearing in mind these were pre telemetry days, and other than a sighting by a postman as she sat on a telegraph pole was unfortunately never seen again.

As well as falcons there have been a number of passage tiercels that have found their way into the older works on falconry due to their prowess in the field. "The Earl" and "The Doctor" were a cast of passage tiercels taken in Holland in 1873 and sent over to England for the Old hawking Club and trained by John Barr. This cast is famous for the only one known to be successfully flown at Lapwings on a regular basis.

"Destiny" was taken in Holland on passage in 1883 and trained by George Oxer. He was flown for seven seasons and took over two hundred head of quarry which included Gulls, Rooks, Magpies, Partridge, Grouse and Pheasant. In the latter part of his career he was flown in a cast with a red tiercel of the year called "Impulse" at Gulls.

On a purely personal basis I have to say that the passage Peregrine, be it falcon or tiercel, are for me the number one and two on the most desirable list of falconry partners. I have been fortunate enough in my long falconry career to have had the pleasure of flying a number of different species of passage falcon ranging from Red Headed Merlin, Lugger and Saker through to Barbary, Red Naped Shaheen and various Peregrine sub species as well as the nominate species itself. I have only had experience of one wild Gyr and that was a haggard Jerkin not a passager. However even above these mightiest of all the falcons I would place the Peregrine in terms of practicality and desirability.

OBTAINING THE PASSAGER

Let me start this chapter by stating categorically that I have never trapped in any way or under any circumstances any raptor of any description in my home country as to do so, certainly for the entirety of my falconry life, has been illegal as well as immoral. There are a considerable number of methods for obtaining a passage falcon and it should be kept very much to the front of the reader's mind that this book is written by someone who has been fortunate enough to visit a great many different countries and cultures in the pursuit of falconry. Accordingly I will set down here the methods I have used myself or seen others use to obtain passage hawks as well as some methods I have never seen used but am aware of. It should be remembered that what is perfectly acceptable and legal in one country may well be frowned on and actually be illegal in another. So, accordingly please note that all the trapping I have been involved in has been perfectly legal in the country in which it was carried out and also, I believe, ethically acceptable. I have also been fortunate enough on several occasions to accompany friends in countries other than Great Britain that have been involved in research work with different species of raptors and accordingly have had the opportunity to trap a number of individuals to ring them, take blood samples, measure and weigh them etc, before releasing them again and letting them continue with their journey.

This chapter is undoubtedly the one that has given me the most trouble with the writing of this book. Not because what I want to say is difficult to put down on paper but rather that there is a question in my head as to whether I should be putting it down at all. I discussed the matter with several friends, who have all been falconers for quite a number of years, and some of whom have flown passage falcons and also with others that have never had the opportunity to do so. Their opinion was unanimously that I should write the chapter and that the very few people in the world who would wish to trap illegally are probably already well versed in the methods that are likely to bring them success. This book will make not an iota of difference to either their knowledge or their moral outlook. By the same reasoning those interested enough to buy and read this book are unlikely to be the sort of people that will go out and act irresponsibly and deliberately outside of the law. So I have included the various ways that I have come across of obtaining a passage falcon other than by simply buying one.

It has to be said that, for me at least, the ultimate falconry experience is to take your own falcon from the wild, train and fly her at quarry and should she eventually become lost then she has only returned to from whence she originally came. Hopefully the falcon will be none the worse for her dalliance in the company of man and may even have gained a little knowledge to add to her store. Some of the most thrilling moments of my life have been to see a particularly beautiful passage falcon, either in flight or at rest, and then within just a very short while, with a minimum of equipment and fuss, she will be in my hands ready to set out on our career together. Whilst locating an eyrie and taking an eyas is exciting and something of a defining moment nothing can compare to taking up a wild falcon, no matter by what method of capture. I have never ever been so calm at that moment as to take a photograph of the falcon before taking her out of the net or off of the harnessed pigeon. The overriding desire is always to ensure the falcon is removed from which ever device ensured her capture and to minimise her stress and also any possible risk of damage to her plumage. It should be remembered the falcon will be trying to foot anything it feels is helping with hindering her bid for freedom so the risk of her inflicting damage on herself as she tries to get free is quite a serious one. Accordingly the falconer should make haste to free the falcon from the method of capture and get her hooded, socked and equipped as quickly and if possible at such times, as calmly as possible.

Probably the method known to just about every falconer in the world is the fantastically intricate and complicated system that was employed by the hawk trappers of Valkenswaard in Holland. However the method they used was also put into practice in various others locations such as Aarendonk in Belgium and also in Norway. Of the famed Dutch trappers it was probably the Mollen family which refined and improved the system over the years to become the apparently effective system it was.

The system required quite a large area to operate in and was truly very intricate in its method of operation. First of all a very crude hut would be constructed out of turfs for the trapper to sit in and work, whilst waiting for the opportunity to present itself to trap a falcon. The Mollens were amongst other things shoemakers and so taking plenty of work to occupy the long hours of waiting would have presented no problem to them. With the hut in place the next step was to erect several twenty foot high poles that were spaced some way apart and in an arc when looked at from the hut. In the top of each pole a pin with an iron ring was inserted. Next a small shelter sufficiently large enough to house a pigeon was constructed out of sods and peat turf approximately thirty feet or so in front of one of the poles. A line ran from the pigeon hut, up over the pole and through the ring, then on down some fifty yards or so away to the hawk trappers hut. When trapping commenced a pigeon fitted with soft leather jesses would be attached to the line and placed inside the hut.

The next pole had a wooden falcon upon it, and the dummy falcon was depicted as if being in flight and ahead of it a short way on the line was a bundle of feathers. From a distance it was meant to represent a falcon chasing a prey item. Again the line from this pole ran back to hawk trappers hut. By pulling on the line the falcon and bundle of feathers could be made to go to ground and into another little sod and peat turf hut and accordingly out of sight of any falcon making her way across the sky to have a look at perhaps the chance of obtaining an easy meal.

Another pigeon was housed in yet another temporary sod and peat turf shelter and this one, fitted with jesses and a line that went back to the trappers hut was the real bait for the approaching falcon. Its line ran along the ground and again passed through the ring that was on top of an iron peg. The pin itself was set right in the middle of the span of bow net when closed. When trapping was under way the bow net would be folded back on itself and clipped back in the ready position. Again a line would run to the trappers hut.

The last crucial element for this set up was a sentinel to take the tedium and human error factor out of the hawk trapper having to be looking skyward all day for the falcons he was intending to try and trap. A mound was constructed from the local abundant material, that is sods and peat turf, and within the mound was an area that a small bird could take refuge in if it felt threatened at any point. Tethered to this mound would be a Butcher Bird or Great Grey Shrike to give it its proper name. Shrikes have incredible eyesight and give very loud and agitated warning of the approach of a raptor. This entire set up would often be repeated at the same sight and so two of everything would be in place and ready to go at the start of the days trapping. With all the lines that ran into the trappers hut it must have resembled a puppeteer's work place inside.

When the Shrike cried out its warning that a falcon was approaching; the wooden falcon and bundle of feathers would be pulled up to the top of the pole and then back down again and away out of sight. As the falcon drew closer to investigate the pigeon concealed in the turf shelter would be hauled to the top of its pole and then allowed to flutter back down and take refuge in its shelter. The falcon would then be overhead supposedly wondering what on earth had happened to its potential prey and it was then that the second pigeon that could be drawn into the bow net would be brought into play. It would flutter and the falcon, if all went to plan, would come down and take her easy prize. As she settled on the pigeon the trapper would draw again gently but firmly on the line attached to the pigeon until it could no longer be drawn. This meant falcon and pigeon were right in centre of the arc that would be covered when the bow release was pulled and this was then done. In an instant the falcon and pigeon were covered with the bow net.

The trapper would leave his hut and as quickly as possible remove the falcon from the net and take her back to the hut. Speed was essential for two reasons. Firstly to minimise the stress to the falcon and get her safely into a manageable condition as quickly as possible. Secondly another falcon may well be within sight and the trapper wouldn't want to scare off a potential second catch of the day. Once back in the hut with the falcon, a rufter hood would be fitted and the falcon placed in a sock. She would then have jesses leash and swivel fitted and the tips of her beak and talons would be clipped back slightly to help reduce the risk of any self induced damage. For those not too sure a rufter hood is a soft loose fitting hood with the back cut away and is purely a temporary measure. The sock is quite literally that and has the toe end cut away. The sock is then rolled down over the body of the falcon acting as a very effective straight jacket. It reduces the risk of feather damage and in combination with the rufter hood serves to keep the falcon quiet and restrained which means the trapper can concentrate on other things and not keep having to attend to her until it is time to head home for the day.

Apparently, to take two falcons in a day with this method, when it was in general use, did happen but only very occasionally whereas by contrast blank days were many indeed. The migration season is a relatively short one and so the huts had to be operational seven days a week throughout its duration otherwise it would not have provided a sufficient income for the hawk trappers to make the whole operation a worthwhile one.

As a curiosity I mention the fact that Edward Clough Newcombe visited Norway in search of Gyr Falcons in eighteen thirty-nine. Newcombe held Gyrs in high esteem and had taken various steps in trying to acquire them. Even to the extent of having handbills printed and issuing them to the captains of whaling ships sailing in the North Sea asking that they take every step possible to help obtain such falcons for him. In the end he went to Norway himself and eventually settled on what he thought would be the most suitable place to give him the success he was after with his trapping expedition. He put in place the following year the building of huts to replicate the Dutch trapping system and in digging the foundations for the new huts the workmen discovered the remains of ancient huts that had been used for the same purpose. In the first year of operation the new huts produced a catch of three Gyr Falcons and the following year, with Dutch falconers operating the trapping system from them, a dozen or so Gyrs were taken. Incidentally all of these Gyrs were sent to the falconers at the Loo Hawking Club and were trained there. Out of this fine collection of Gyrs only two, a Gyr and a Jerkin, turned out to be good ones. One was trained by James Bots and the other by Adrian Mollen. The Gyr Falcon in question is often thought to be the famous “Zoe”.

This highly intricate system of catching falcons was recreated a few years ago in Aarendonk in Belgium as part of the town’s celebration of its eight hundred years history. I made the journey across to Belgium so as to take advantage of a really good opportunity to study a life size working model of the method. Seeing a model in a museum or drawings can obviously never be the same as seeing the real thing. I have to say my abiding memory, still to this day, is just how complicated the system was and the numerous amount of potential opportunities for there to be a snag in its operation and therefore perhaps a trapping loss. Having said that the system was undoubtedly an effective one in its day or else it simply would not have been in use for so long and another method would have replaced it. However, I really do wonder if the same number of falcons could not have been taken without the vastly complex and elaborate system employed by the Mollen family and others. With the Shrike as a sentinel and a decent bow net with a bait pigeon or better still a harnessed pigeon on a line then surely it would have been possible to achieve the same, or dare I say it better, results.

My own opinion is that at this moment in time that this book is being written the two most effective methods of trapping falcons are either by Do-Gazza or by the use of a harnessed pigeon. The Do-Gazza, which is to all intents and purposes a vertical net that will collapse in on any falcon that impacts with it, would be very much my second choice if I was trapping falcons and the original version of the trap really is a crude unsophisticated device. The net as used in Pakistan and India is a large square of mesh, approximately six foot by six foot, which is made up of two inch diamond mesh, and the material used is thick brown cotton. The net is attached to two vertical poles by means of a series of rings and the bottom is weighted with a bag of sand or some other method. The idea is that a bait bird, such as a pigeon or a dove, is tethered directly in front of the net. As a falcon stoops at the bait, no matter which side she comes from, she will hit the net and it will fold in on her. Should she manage somehow to get both her wings free the weighted addition to the bottom of the net will not stop her dead in her tracks but will help absorb some of the shock and prevent her from flying away. A much more effective net can be made from plaited nylon and with much larger diamonds within the netting, say three or even four inches. Instead of using vertical poles and the net permanently attached by a series of rings the net can be clipped to the poles at each corner with detachable clips, such as used on bait lines for fishing or even those that allow the lure to detach from a kite when a falcon is flown at it. Again the bottom of the net would be weighted to prevent the possibility of the falcon flying off with the net wrapped around her. But the weight would be a trailing one, such as a thick rope or not too heavy chain. This would ensure that there was a considerable give at the moment of impact should a falcon be taken in the net.

Using nets is a tried and trusted method of trapping passage falcons but by their very nature are prone to getting tangled and being realistic are somewhat fiddly to set absolutely correctly. Having got the net set up just so, then the trapper has to have a bait bird positioned just so that a falcon striking them is caught but not close enough to the net that they can cause its collapse. It is not a quick reaction method of trapping falcons and still requires a considerably greater slice of luck than the more effective method I have always preferred to use.

For me the easiest to use, most successful method of taking falcons on passage is without doubt the harnessed pigeon. Nothing comes close to the success rate of this method and if its deployment brings up a falcon that is interested enough to venture over to have a look then nine times out of ten it will result in success and the taking of that falcon. The harnessed pigeon is exactly what it says it is. A pigeon is fitted with a harness that allows the wings through the body of the device and then fastens round the front on the breast of the pigeon. Across the flat surface of the harness, which lays on the back of the pigeon, the area is literally festooned with nylon nooses. From the front of the harness a line some five to six metres long extends and is fitted to a dragged weight which

Karl Mollen with Passage Falcon

is heavy enough to stop the falcon making off with it but sufficiently light to not pull the falcon up instantly. This shock could well prove to be far too severe for the falcon and accordingly a method of minimising that shock is employed.

A very simple and truly effective weight is easily made out in the field. Take a one third of a litre plastic drinks bottle and put a small hole in the cap. Only just large enough to pass the line through that is attached to the harness on the pigeon. Knot the line inside the cap so as it cannot pull through and then simply fill the bottle with sand or earth to act a dragged weight. Do not under any circumstance use water as this will seep out with use and thereby diminish its drag factor. So now we have the most effective trap that I know of consisting merely of a pigeon, harness, plastic bottle, line and sand or earth. Depending on where the falconer is trapping putting the trap into operation varies very little. Whether it is beach trapping, working a pylon or telegraph pole line the method is more or less the same. Let us take as our example beach trapping for Tundra Peregrines as they head down the Eastern coast of North America and Mexico making their way to Patagonia. The first thing to remember with beach peregrines is that they rest on the ground. Normally the environment in which they are found is more or less a treeless one and so there is no alternative perch to the ground itself. However Tundra's will avail themselves of any perch that is readily available such as a decent sized piece of drift wood or old fence posts.

One of the places I used to trap, with appropriate licences let me re-iterate, was on the eastern coast of Mexico and the beach itself was more than twenty kilometres long, and varied in how far it went back from between one and three kilometres. At the height of the migration it would not be unusual to see in excess of fifteen different peregrines in a morning and afternoon session of the same day. The reason a day would be split into sessions was to avoid trying to trap when the heat of the day was at its highest and any capture of a passager would therefore subject it to an extra element of danger, which is heat stroke. So the normal routine, particularly when trapping for research, would be active from seven am until around ten am depending on temperature then again from around four pm till approximately six pm. When trapping a falcon under licence for falconry we would take just one harnessed pigeon. When doing research work we would always strive to have two harnessed pigeons ready to go because you just never know what you may come across.

The method of operation when deploying a harnessed pigeon really couldn't be any simpler and yet it is stunningly effective. We would drive slowly along the beach, stopping every three hundred yards or so and would check the area with decent binoculars. If nothing was seen, then move on another three hundred yards and so on. When a sitting falcon was spotted the next move was to determine was it a passage or a haggard falcon and indeed was it a falcon or a tiercel. This wasn't normally too difficult as Tundra Peregrines are pretty tolerant of vehicles and unless you get too close are not overly bothered if a car appears a just a couple of hundred yards away, that is providing you do not get out of the car or make too much movement within the car. Also, time of the migration helps considerably if you are in an area when the falcons are passing through as opposed to an area where they intend to settle in for the next five months or so. Migration follows a very rough pattern in that adult falcons migrate first followed by adult tiercels and then the young of the year. Now this isn't a strictly adhered to edict of nature, but it is surprising how you tend to see one sex and life stage of a peregrine at a time when they are migrating through an area.

Obviously when helping with research work the whole of the migration was of interest and so there was no specific time that was considered ideal for trapping and the rest of the migration was not. For the falconer with a licence to take a passage falcon then obviously the timing is crucial. No good going to the beach to trap when there are only haggards if you are too early and almost only passage tiercels if you are too late. So let's assume we are on the beach, a passage falcon has been spotted resting on a piece of driftwood and she is a falcon we would like to take. We spot, if we can, the size of her crop. If she has one we do not give up unless it is anything other than a bulging one which would indicate she ate in the last hour or so. It is a tendency for people, even experienced falconers, to forget that just as with any other predator, the passage falcon is an opportunist feeder and will take advantage of a situation that presents itself if it is one that could prove beneficial to her. I have in fact caught passage peregrines that did indeed have a full crop but were perfectly willing to still make a kill and cram just a little more in or even perhaps cache the kill.

It also should be borne in mind haggard and passage falcons react differently to each other when attacking the harnessed pigeon presented to them. A passage falcon will as often as not come straight in and quite literally grab the pigeon immediately. Occasionally, a passager will make a low pass or two and then fully commit to grabbing the pigeon. The foolhardiness of youth and the drive of hunger or the chance of an apparently easy meal are obviously guiding the thought process of the falcon. Whereas, with the haggard she will make a number of shallow stoops at the pigeon and if the pigeon stops fluttering and sits on the ground the haggard falcon will often fly away. It seems to know that the fact the pigeon won't fly means that something is out of the ordinary and it decides discretion is the better part of valour. All the time the pigeon flutters, I assume the falcon thinks that the pigeon must be injured and therefore the falcon is merely awaiting the right moment to grab it.

Having spotted the falcon we wish to trap, we now drive gently to within approximately a hundred yards of it and slowly turn the vehicle so that it is sideways on to the falcon. On the side furthest away from her the harnessed pigeon is tossed out of the car and then we drive slowly away from the falcon revealing a pigeon that cannot seem to fly off of the beach and could present the opportunity of an easy meal. We pull back a couple of hundred yards and then turn the vehicle around so as to be facing the falcon and the pigeon. In practically every case the falcon will already be in the air and flying at the pigeon. The pigeon will go to fly and because of the restriction will prescribe an arc in the air and normally land on the ground again. This usually proves to be just too tempting for the falcon and it rushes in and binds to the pigeon, fluttering very quickly to earth with it. Being a Tundra Peregrine it doesn't seek a tree in which to eat its prize but settles happily on the sand. The pigeon is despatched and the falcon then has a good look round to make sure no Red Tailed Hawk or Ferruginous is on the lookout ready to either steal its meal or indeed kill it.

This is the moment when the falconer must be patient and watch the falcon on her prize through binoculars. We must wait till the falcon goes about the business of pluming and eating her meal. She needs to be well and truly caught before we rush in and make an attempt to finally get her in our hands. When we feel she is well and truly occupied with her meal and has shifted herself a couple of times, we start the vehicle and edge very gently towards her. As she becomes aware of us getting ever closer she will become nervous and actually reach a point where she wants to step off of the pigeon in readiness for taking off. It is at this moment that we can see if she is indeed noosed or not. If she steps clear from the pigeon, then clearly she is not and the vehicle needs to be put in reverse and back off gently to its original parked position and then later repeat the process when we think she is noosed. If however she cannot step off of the pigeon and her attempts to do so result in the pigeon being dragged, then it is a case jumping out of the vehicle and running to her at full speed, and take her in our hands to stop her struggling against the nooses. A rough fitting old hood will be slipped on and a sock rolled down over her body so as to restrain her. Her toes will be freed from the nooses and for the few seconds it takes anklets, jesses, leash and swivel fitted. On such occasions I find false aylmeri invaluable. In a matter of just a few minutes the falcon is equipped and safely removed from the harness. If you are fortunate to have a friend helping get them to take plenty of pictures, this moment with this falcon will never be repeated and the memory should live with you for the rest of your life, but even so it is nice to have some photographs of this really special event. In your hands now will be the prize that generations of falconers around the world have held in the highest esteem.

I have had many incidents that I feel make interesting anecdotes when out trapping and shall recall just a few to give a flavour of what can happen when trapping and help to make up memories that will thankfully live in the mind forever.

On one occasion I was trapping on a beach in Mexico for research purposes and myself and my companion had just banded and released a fine haggard peregrine who was running a little late regarding natures schedule and was within the time frame where we were finding mainly passage falcons at that point. The apparent tameness of Tundra Peregrines is difficult to try and explain to those that have never had dealings with them and they tolerate man and his presence in a way I haven't encountered with any other species of falcon. As any trapped and banded Tundra was released we would unfailingly throw out the body of the pigeon that had been instrumental in taking her. Falcons always come back, with the exception of very few cases, to claim their prize and carry it off despite the fact it was used to trap them. The haggard in question was making off with her meal when two passagers appeared from nowhere and started putting in short stoops at her in an attempt to rob her of her meal. We immediately threw out another harnessed pigeon to try and deflect them from her and quickly made up another and threw it out as well. Both passagers left the older falcon and returned to take what for them was going to be a far easier option. The falcons piled straight in, but strangely into the same pigeon leaving the second pigeon free. However not for long as out of nowhere came a third falcon and bound to the second pigeon.

Now myself and companion where in something of a quandary, we had three passage peregrines noosed at once when the system we operated between us was so quick and effective because we worked in unison on one falcon at a time. We had honed and refined this method we used to get the required procedure done and the falcon on its way again in the minimum possible amount of time. Keeping stress levels for the falcon as low as possible are obviously a very important criteria. In the situation in which we found ourselves experience took over and we as calmly as possible removed each falcon from the harness, hooded and socked them and then dealt with the three individuals as quickly as possible. I have to say it did cross my mind shortly after the event that even the Mollens, with all their combined years of trapping experience, had in all probability never seen something like that.

Another time I remember when the surf was running quite high as it crashed against the beach where we were trapping. In the troughs running parallel to the beach a poor Cattle Egret was trying to evade the unwanted attentions of no less than five separate passage falcons. The Egret flew as close to the water as it possibly dare and probably only had literally inches to spare between itself and the sea. The falcons were putting in short sharp stoops at the Egret but wouldn't quite commit that last little bit, obviously as they also feared what could be a watery end. My companion and I were ready to trap; accordingly we tossed out two harnessed pigeons and instantly all five passage falcons switched their intentions from the Egret to our tastier and hopefully drier option. The Egret took full advantage of the sudden switch in the attention of the falcons and made good its escape.

Two falcons were taken almost immediately and my companion and I rushed out to take them off of the harnesses and process them, band them and release them. As we did so we obviously tossed out their pigeons for them as we always did and one of the other falcons came straight in for a look and we quickly harnessed another pigeon and took her as well. Now this was a falcon I would have bet good money against successfully trapping as she had seen her two companions taken and temporarily ending up in the hands of humans.

Another time we were trapping on a beach and spotted a haggard and a passage sitting on two old fence poles that were only some ten or twelve feet apart. The haggard had a simply fit to burst full crop and the passage falcon no crop at all. We decided to try for the passage and went through the ritual of approaching with the vehicle, turning away and then hey presto there was a pigeon the falcon hadn't seen previously. As we pulled away we looked in the rear view mirror and a falcon was already on the pigeon. We turned the vehicle slowly around to observe the falcon and try and determine when she was actually caught and we should move in. Much to our surprise the original haggard and passage falcons were still sitting on the respective posts and this was a falcon we just hadn't seen that was obviously perched nearby. The amazing point to this anecdote is that while we took the passager from the net and did what we had to do and then released her with her pigeon, the young falcon on the post watched the whole procedure with one foot tucked up and didn't fly off. The haggard falcon had darted the second we got out of the car, which is obviously the sort of behaviour you would expect.

I have to say my companion and I were a little troubled at the lack of excitement in this falcon regarding the pigeon and the fact that even two humans, less than a hundred yards from her, had not caused her to take flight or indeed even upset her rest. It was getting close to the end of our morning trapping session as the heat of the day was increasing rapidly and Red Tails and Ferruginous Hawks were thermaling, never a good time to trap. We decided to take our lunch at that point and parked our vehicle so we could sit in the little shade it provided and watch the falcon that was giving us cause for concern. As we sat and ate lunch and drank copious amounts of cold water the falcon seemed to switch on and suddenly started to vigorously preen and get herself into flying order. She then took off and in a determined manner rung up to a decent height, certainly six or seven hundred feet, and then put in a very long shallow angled stoop. We lost sight of her and the end result of the stoop and at least we were heartened by the fact that there was clearly nothing wrong with her and we had mistaken tolerance of humans on her part as sickness of some kind. It is all too easy to forget that on the Tundra, in all probability, the vast majority of the falcons from there only ever see humans when on migration. As we were discussing this aspect of falcon life our passager returned to her post with a Green Sand Piper in her foot proving once and for all she was in the very rudest of health.

When trapping passage falcons at the height of migration, it is all too easy to get lulled into a false sense of lethargy when it comes to the mental process. I find I have a tendency to get so absorbed in what I am doing I almost lose track of what is around me, other than falcons. I once threw out a harnessed pigeon for a falcon I had spotted and driving away and looking in the rear view mirror was surprised to see a large brown raptor, which clearly wasn't a peregrine grappling with our pigeon. On getting back I discovered I had in fact caught a Marsh Harrier and it was not overly keen on me helping it out of the nooses that held it. That one raptor inflicted more bites on me than any other bird of prey I have ever trapped.

As a falconer I have always loved Prairie Falcons and have a real liking for them, both in the wild and to hunt with. On one particular trapping afternoon however the sheer tenacity and braveness of one made me momentarily have

Tundra Peregrine

doubts regarding my fondness for them. The morning session of this day had been a staggeringly good one with a fair number of passage falcons caught and rung in the duration of it. We began the afternoon session with just four pigeons left but that meant we had the possibility of trapping four more falcons in that session, that is, if we could find them.

Almost immediately on setting out we came across what can only be described as truly beautiful blonde Tundra sitting on some driftwood. Through binoculars she was simply gorgeous and I was convinced she had to be the lightest coloured Tundra I had ever seen. I was really looking forward to getting a close up and personal look at her as we processed her. The harnessed pigeon was deployed in the normal manner and our Tundra reacted almost immediately and started making her way over. Unfortunately before she could quite get to it a Prairie Falcon appeared out of the sky and really harassed the youngster very hard indeed until it got to the point where the youngster thought better of the situation and flew away. To add insult to injury the Prairie Falcon put in a blinding stoop at our pigeon and, quite literally, decapitated it. To add further insult the prairie didn't want our pigeon but merely flew to some tussocks in the dunes a few yards away and settled there.

Another passager had obviously witnessed the proceedings and expressing the nature of being a falcon that is somewhat confused, landed on the sand a few feet away from our dead pigeon. Instantly this youngster landed, the Prairie Falcon was off in attack mode again and eventually chased the young falcon away. This seemed to satisfy the Prairie's lust for a bit of a scrap with other falcons and it rung up and drifted off, last seen only barely visible to the naked eye. We retrieved our pigeon and harness and having reset the harness on a fresh pigeon started our search for falcons again. We had barely driven ten minutes when we spotted the particularly blonde Tundra from the earlier incident. She still didn't have a crop and so we deployed our pigeon in the normal manner. The Tundra took to the air and made a couple of tentative passes at the pigeon before coming in hard and fast and taking it. In fact it hit the pigeon so hard it lifted it clear of the ground and falcon and pigeon came to earth around ten feet away. This falcon surely had to be noosed, however we sat patiently in the vehicle waiting for the moment that we would be convinced she was actually noosed and suddenly our contemplation was rudely shattered by the loud angry hecking of a falcon.

The Prairie Falcon was back and angry at the presence of the Tundra. To our astonishment the Tundra wasn't noosed and made off with the Prairie in hot pursuit. We watched them both fly completely out of sight into the distance. I got out of our vehicle to go and retrieve our pigeon and we removed the harness so as to reset it on one of two remaining pigeons. Having reflected on the situation we decided to drive for at least a mile away from the direction we had seen the Prairie disappearing before we tried again. Very soon we found a passage falcon and deployed our last but one pigeon and the falcon reacted well and came in. She bound to the pigeon and, as usual, we waited to see the moment we knew for sure she was caught. All of a sudden the falcon tried to take off and it was evident by her failure to do so she was indeed noosed. She had tried to take off not because of us in the vehicle, but because the Prairie Falcon was back and attacking. We had to rush to her to stop the Prairie pressing home her attack and even as we carried out our ringing process she kept circling and hecking not too far away.

Having rung the falcon we didn't want to release her immediately, as we thought the Prairie really might press home the attack and hurt, if not actually kill her. So we took the young falcon to the car for a few minutes and covered her head with a towel to keep stress as low as possible. When the Prairie flew off we released the falcon and gave her the pigeon that had brought her in. Enough was enough for that day, we admitted defeat and to the fact that we had been removed from the beach by a Prairie Falcon. If nothing else you have to admire their spirit.

There are other ways to trap hawks and two of which I have not tried. One out of the fact that other methods I have employed have proved so successful and the other because I think it's a potential disaster waiting to happen and have seen firsthand the results of it going wrong. I refer to the use of a Barak hawk, where a hawk of a lesser importance to the trapper is released in sight of the falcon he wishes to trap, with a bundle of feathers festooned with nooses attached to its jesses. The lesser hawk has the potential to be killed, fly off and die a miserable death on its own, handicapped by what it carries, or indeed for both bait hawk and trapped hawk to fly off out of the reach of the trappers and thereby perish. I am sure, that like nearly everything in life, there is a right way and wrong way to carry out this method of trapping and perhaps done correctly there is a minimal risk but there would still be too great a risk of harm to the Barak hawk itself and that would prevent me from ever giving it a try.

The other method I haven't tried is Paddam Nooses. This is a series of large nooses, some six inches in diameter, arranged in a circle where the nooses stand vertically and each noose very slightly overlaps its neighbour. The circle is approximately three feet in diameter and in the centre is tethered a bait bird appropriate for the species that is being trapped, normally a pigeon or a dove. The idea is that a falcon on taking the bait bird will get itself snared by at least one noose and the more it struggles, the more it should become entangled. Hardly a rapidly erected device when out in the field and one that would probably be more suited, in a modified form, to trapping smaller falcons.

A method I have tried, but again, at least to me, smacks of being over complicated for the sake of it, is the noose carpet. A tethered, unharnessed, pigeon is placed where a passage falcon can see it. The scenario is supposed to unfold in that the falcon comes in and kills the pigeon. She is allowed to start to plume her prize and then driven off of it by the trapper who then lays a wire covered frame made of chicken wire or twiweld and which is itself festooned with nooses, over the prey. This is then pegged down over the corpse of the pigeon and the trapper then retires to observe. If the falcon is still in the vicinity she will return to her kill and get noosed as she tries to get at her prey. I have only seen this system actually put into practice on the one occasion and it was done so more for my benefit than anything else. The intended target was a passage Lanner Falcon and I have to say that although we caught her I was singularly unimpressed with the method for three simple reasons. Firstly she has already come in and taken a tethered pigeon and yet we drove her off with the potential risk of her going altogether. Secondly this particular lanner got her beak as well as her feet caught in the nooses as she tried to actually eat her prey. Thirdly as the falcon was caught in this totally defenceless position we had to actually race a family of Banded Mongooses to get to her before they did. She would not have stood a chance if we had lost the race. It seemed to me an inefficient way to trap falcons and one that potentially put them at great and totally unnecessary risk.

The final method to be described in these pages is a method which I have been fortunate enough to try first hand, but very unfortunately only on one single occasion, is quite literally by hand. I have no idea what the correct title for this type of trapping is but perhaps it should be "The gently and stealthily approach". It is only really applicable to beach trapping and requires patience and trust in your companion. A shallow grave is dug in the sand and the falconer lies in it on his back. He is then covered over with sand with the exception of his head. This is covered with a wicker basket or similar and only protrudes from the sand sufficiently to enable the falconer to see a little around him and of course breathe without taking in mouthfuls of sand. A pigeon tethered by means of soft jesses and a line is given to the falconer and the line is tied around the wrist of the falconer. The wrist is retracted under the sand so all that is visible is a little uneven ground and a pigeon fluttering on the end of a relatively short line.

It is then simply a case of waiting for a falcon to take the pigeon and as soon as she is engaged in pluming and eating her prey the line is gradually drawn towards the hand of the falconer. Because the falcon cannot see the falconer or anything else nearby hence she will not be alarmed and simply hold onto the pigeon and treat it as if it was still struggling. With care the falconer can slowly and steadily draw the falcon sufficiently close to his hand that he can feel the legs of the falcon and when he does, he grabs her and emerges with his valuable prize from the sand. As to the trust in your companions the last thing you want is to be buried just beneath the surface of the sand and some people looking to have recreation time on the beach drive over you!

Whatever method the falconer uses to obtain his passage falcon there really is no feeling like it in the world or at least that is how it is for me.

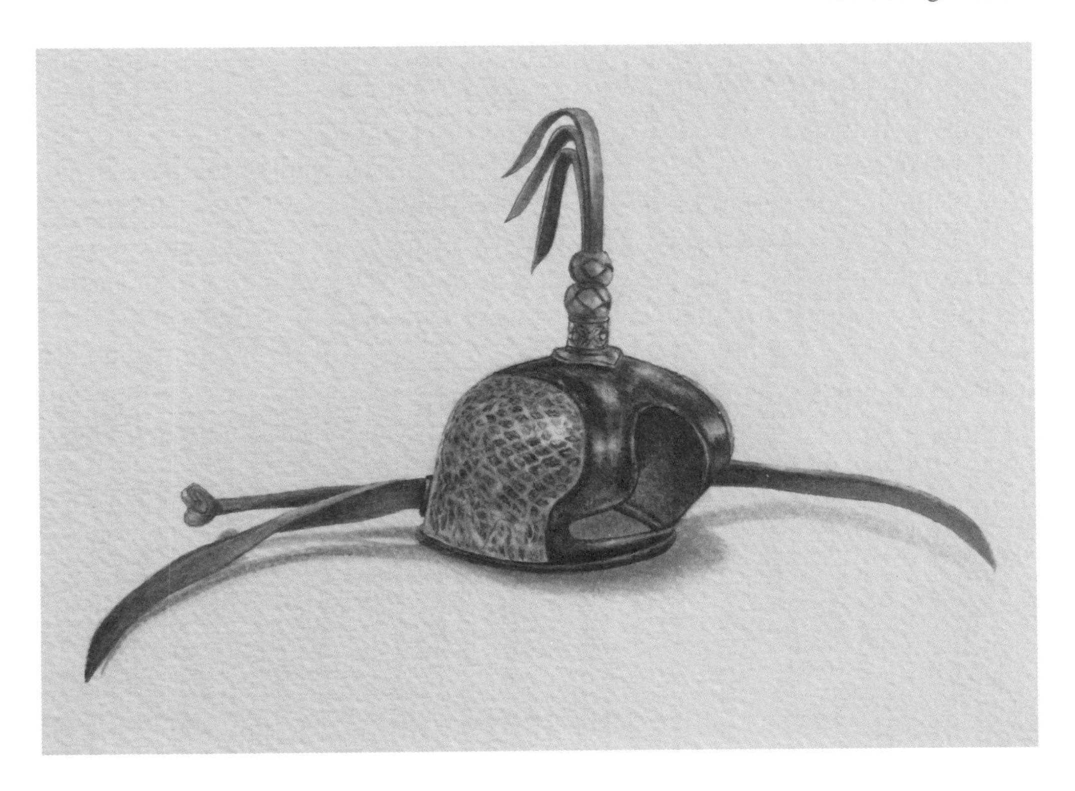

HOODING

A falcon wears a hood for a variety of reasons which all realistically come down to giving the falconer control over any given situation that he or she and the falcon may encounter. The hood can prevent the falcon getting frightened, bating unnecessarily, trying to get at quarry it has no chance of catching and damaging itself whilst being transported. The fact that a falcon will, on the vast majority of occasions, calm down almost instantly when a hood is put on, even a wild taken freshly trapped falcon, then it is more than obvious that the hood is an essential piece of equipment, not only in the early days of training but for the rest of its working life. Just imagine trying to train a falcon without using the hood, at the same time try and envisage the condition of its plumage had such a thing been attempted. However, the hood is an essential tool throughout the flying career of the falcon and its usage, other than perhaps for those that moult their falcons loose in an aviary, will be an everyday fact of life. There are several basic styles of hoods which more or less come down to three distinct types. There are numerous variations on a theme but realistically we are talking three main body types.

The Dutch, which is a three piece hood sewn inside out then dried and shaped on a block. This style of hood used to have a straight cut slot as a beak opening and therefore tended to have a very poor fit around the face of the falcon. Worse it could lead to rubbing of the cere as well as the base of the beak and cause irritation to the falcon. The skin around the base of the beak is apparently very tender and a heavy hood resting on this area can very soon teach a falcon to resent the hood with a passion. Who wouldn't resent being made to wear shoes on a daily basis that were a size too small and hurt the feet? Also the hood constantly rubbing at the tender areas of flesh will eventually cause the skin to break and each time the hood is re-applied these lesions will be opened again and all too soon will become infected. The traditional Dutch hood has baize cloth eye pieces and the colour of these eye pieces denoted the quarry the falcon was flown at. Red would be for a game hawk, green a rook hawk and purple a heron hawk. A falcon that had successfully taken heron would have the plume of the hood made from the throat feathers of the heron. Otherwise the plume on the Dutch hoods was traditional cockerel feathers. Nowadays the cloth eye pieces have mostly been done away with and the beak opening has also been greatly modified to ensure a much better fit and not to touch the cere or tender flesh around the beak at all. Because the modified hood itself will sit back further onto the face of the falcon, now it is also easier to get a much better fit all round than with the previous style of slot beak opening. Techniques have altered greatly in the actual process of hood making, as have some of the materials used, and modern hoods are much lighter and hold their shape better that their counterparts from years gone by.

The Arab Style which is a one piece hood with the back of the hood not cut in any way and so instead of having two edges that butt up to each other when closed the back gathers together when closed, looking very similar to pleats on a ladies skirt. These are very functional hoods and tend to be light in weight but in the days of leather hood braces they had a tendency to come open just a little bit. This very slight opening of the braces would allow the hood to move forward a fraction and thereby allow a little light in through the front of the hood. This would inevitably set the falcon off scratching at the hood and then it may well have actually succeeded in getting the hood off which could have had disastrous consequences.

The last is the Anglo Indian which again is a one piece hood but it has a slit up the back so as to meet exactly at the back when closed. This was a combination of two different designs. The original Indian hood did not open or close but was slipped onto the head of the falcon but the falcon with a deft movement of her foot could just as easily hook it back off again. So a system was devised whereby the hood pattern was adjusted to have a slit up the back and then braces were fitted as on the Dutch style of hood. The best of both world combinations works very well. Anglo Indian hoods are utilitarian and practical and can endure all sorts of mistreatments such as repeatedly being stuffed in a pocket when a falcon is flown. The design of the hood includes a throat lash which passes in and out of the hood around its lower circumference. So many falconers fail to realise this lash is not decorative but actually an adjustment for the hood. It can either be tightened slightly or just as easily slackened off a little. The adjustment brought about is not great but is often sufficient to ensure the hood fits properly. The Anglo Indian style hood is certainly the lightest of the three basic designs and is something in the order of half the price of the other two designs because of the amount of time it takes to make. There are some exceedingly skilful hood makers around. David Masters in Scotland has now devised a method of making blocked Anglo Indian hoods and they are simply superb hoods made to a very high standard and, more importantly, they fit exceedingly well.

If you are lucky enough to own or get to have a good look at a hood made before the nineteen thirties you will realise just how much hood making, in terms of materials, fit and finesse, has changed and very much changed for the better. The hoods themselves are much lighter and actually fit well. The beak opening has changed from the slot to a keyhole shape, as already mentioned, but this has undoubtedly saved the lives of a number of falcons. With the slot the falcon could not cast or even be sick through it, it simply didn't allow the beak to open sufficiently. With the modern key-hole shape a falcon can cast without problem and should the occasion arise, is able to physically be sick through it. Neither of these things is desirable but better that if they do occur they pass off without further incident.

A major step forward with modern hoods is the use of Gortex braces instead of leather ones. Leather braces on a hood have always been problematical in that sooner or later they slide against each other and the falconer will find that the hood does not stay completely closed anymore and therefore is no longer fit for the job it was designed for. Also when leather braces get truly wet that are virtually impossible to pull apart and you always feel like you are putting the life of your falcon in danger trying to prize them apart. On more than one occasion I have been caught in a downpour out on a grouse moor and as a result on the ensuing soaking have had to cut the braces of the hood to get it off. Then off course you have to re-brace the thing as soon as possible to get it back into service.

This is going to seem an absolutely ridiculous thing to put into print but I am afraid it has to be when I say the most obvious thing about a hood is that it should fit well. However falconry constantly teaches me that there are things that need to be explained or mentioned and I am afraid this is one of them. The amount of times I have been shown a falcon or hawk in its newly acquired perfect fitting hood and then simply pulled it off, without striking the braces, simply don't bear thinking about. With the hooded falcon sitting on the gloved fist take hold of the hood by the plume and very gently but with a constant pressure pull it downwards towards the feet of the falcon. You will be amazed how many times the hood will simply come off. Obviously if you meet resistance stop and acknowledge that the hood does fit. By the same token it is also amazing just how many falcons have a small degree of vision wearing their hoods and most are constantly bothered by it. That seeing something but not quite being able to see it properly must drive them mad.

The beak opening of the hood can be easily modified if the fit is not exact and does lightly touch at some point around the base of the beak. Merely wet the hood or smear a little F10 cream on the inside of the opening, and I really do mean a tiny amount, just enough to make a discernible covering. Then pop the hood on and close it with the braces, leave for a few seconds and then remove again. Where the hood is touching will show up very clearly and then this area can be gently taken back or enlarged a little with a scalpel. Always err on the side of caution and take a very little off each time. Better to take not quite enough and have to repeat the process once or twice than take a larger amount straight out and find you have taken too much. After all you cannot put any material back but you can always trim a little more. If you cut back too far the hood is ruined.

A hood that does not fit properly is simply of no use what so ever and no falconer would be able to relax knowing that a falcon he has left hooded may well be able to get the hood off is she really tries hard. This being never truer than if she has been left in the proximity of other falcons. If she does manage to get her hood off another falcon may well pay with its life due to the fact that a hood that fitted correctly wasn't used. So it pays to take time and care when selecting a hood and ensuring you get exactly what you are after. If you make your own hoods and end up with one that fits all your requirements then my advice would be to immediately make another one as a spare. If you purchase your hoods from equipment suppliers and get exactly what you are after then invest in a spare as soon as possible. It may well pay dividends in the long run.

Obviously a hood that is too tight will be physically uncomfortable for the falcon and she will scratch at it and try and remove it repeatedly and the falconer should be aware it is too tight by several factors. It will not close completely at the back; it will touch the soft skin around the base of the beak and will be plainly something the falcon is desperate to rid herself of. It wouldn't take a great deal of usage of such an ill fitting hood to make a falcon hood shy, a simply awful trait to have to deal with on a daily basis. A hood that lets in a

Hooding Sakret

chink of light can very quickly turn a falcon that has been calm and placid when hooded into a very restless one and a jumper. A vice which once learnt seems to continue even when a correctly fitting hood is then used. A jumper will always prove to be a nightmare whether on a cadge, travelling box, screen perch, shelf perch or indoor block. In no time at all her plumage will show all too clearly the effect of her restlessness when hooded. The hood really is such an important piece of equipment for the falconer to have at his disposal and, as with all equipment; he should strive to use only the best both in terms of quality and fit.

The actual process of hooding is equally important and must be a calm, smooth operation that causes the falcon minimum stress. I say minimum because in the early days of training the hand of a human coming so close will still be something that causes the falcon concern, so all the more reason to be gentle in your actions but at the same time positive and decisive. Good hooding ability in a falconer has often been compared to "good hands" in skilled horseman. Blaine quotes a saying that is not attributed to any one in particular but is never the less absolutely correct in what it says. "No man can claim to be a master of hawks until he is master of the art of hooding; he who has perfected himself in this art has gained the whole secret of the control of his falcon". A fresh falcon fears what she sees and to be able to quickly and smoothly allay the fear by putting a hood on her is something of a gift for the falconer. By means of the hood the falconer can reduce a creature that is on the verge of being panic stricken to one that returns instantly to a passive disposition. Hooded, the falcon is once again calm and it should not be forgotten that carriage in the hood will help with her overall manning.

There are two ways to hold the hood when about to put it on the head of the falcon. The first is to hold the hood in the palm of the hand with the beak opening facing the ball of the thumb and the plume held between thumb and forefinger. The first and second fingers of the hand are placed at the back of the hood and holding it almost vertically the hood is placed onto the head of the falcon in a short arc like movement. The beak will have passed through the appropriate opening and the hood itself should fall snugly into place when released. The braces can then be pulled closed.

The second way is to hold the hood by the plume between the thumb and forefinger. This is the method I much prefer and one which seems to result in me being able to hood a falcon smoothly. The hood is brought to the falcon at slightly below her own head level and then rolled up and over into place in one smooth movement. As well as holding the hood correctly it is also important to hold yourself correctly. You want to make the whole operation go as smoothly as possible and it is attention to detail that is the key to success. When your falcon is nicely settled on the fist bring your left arm so that it is across your body and the falcon is directly facing you with her head at about the height of your chin. Her head will ideally be about nine inches or so from your face and this will mean that once the hood is in place it will be a simple matter to lean forward and take one set of braces in your teeth, the other set in your right hand and then close the hood. As you go to close the hood lower your own head slightly so that you are pulling the braces away from the body of the hood and in a slightly downward manner. This will often prevent the hawk from flicking it off just before you have closed the hood and will also ensure the hood sits back fully on the neck of the hawk.

There is a little trick which may prove useful if you have a falcon with a tendency to get the hood off before you get a chance to do the braces up. As soon as the hood is in place slide your fingers from the plume down to the braces. Take the long brace of the right hand side of the hood as you look at it, where it emerges from the hood, between your index finger and thumb. Whilst your forefinger presses gently against the body of the hood, where the braces are attached, pull the brace with your fingers. The result of this is that the hood will effectively half close. This will make it very difficult for the hawk to flick it off. When she has had a few moments to settle you can then lean forward and take both sets of braces in fingers and teeth, in the more conventional method, and finish closing the hood properly.

Let me just emphasise that the hooding should be a calm and smooth operation designed to put the falcon into, what is for her, a calm place for a while. Accordingly she should never be bludgeoned into wearing it or man handled in any way to get the hood in place. I have seen falcons with the hood eventually wrestled onto their heads then have their heads pushed forward by the forefinger of the falconer applying pressure to the back of the head. I have seen falcons grabbed by the legs and physically restrained in this undignified manner to get the hood on. Both methods are hardly likely to endear the

Hooded Jerkin

presence of the falconer to the falcon or indeed enamour her to the idea of being hooded. As frustrating as some falcons can be in the early days it is normally patience and calm repetition that wins the day. As the falcon progresses with her training and her weight is more in line with what it will be when flying, I am sure it will be found that she is more responsive in general so hooding, if in the least problematical, should also improve. However let me say I have yet to come across a freshly trapped passage falcon that was not good to the hood right from the word go. I am stressing the word freshly here, as a trapped passager that has been through a hawk dealers hands may well have been made hood shy by ignorance or simply the dealer not particularly caring as they know the falcon will be moving on shortly; but then the manners of passage and haggard falcons are always very good especially when compared to the average eyass.

When it comes to unhooding the falcon, ensure that your approach and actions are just as calm and relaxed as if hooding her. Position the falcon correctly and then strike the braces on the hood. Do not then instantly remove the hood. Leave the hood in position with the braces struck for a few seconds and then smoothly remove it. If you hurriedly remove the hood each time the braces are struck the falcon will soon learn to anticipate the moment and when she feels you take hold of the braces she will become restless on the fist or worse still bate in anticipation. This is a bad lesson that can be learnt very quickly if you strike the hood; then snatch it off in anticipation of casting her off at quarry. If it means missing a flight because you don't get the hood off in two seconds flat, then just accept the fact and move on. There will be plenty more slips throughout your hawking association. Always remember to be smooth and positive in your actions when hooding and unhooding your falcon. Take great care to avoid making a falcon in the least hood shy, it does not take too many negative experiences to bring this about but is a condition that can prove almost impossible to correct.

A great many falconry books end their chapter or section on hooding with a long and difficult to read quotation from Edmund Bert. It is difficult to read because it is in Elizabethan English and the method described of making a hawk to the hood was also specifically written for those that trained passage Goshawks. I do not recommend the method related in the book as it involves teaching the hawk to put its head in the hood by the use of food. As mentioned in the chapter on manning I never ever want a hawk of mine to feed through the hood or to think there is the opportunity to feed through the hood. Edmund Bert was obviously a superbly skilful falconer and had probably forgotten more about falconry than I will ever know. But on this one point I dare to differ in my opinion.

MANNING AND TAMING

"I have knowne many Falconers that never make their hawkes to tyre, saying that it is but a custom, and needelesse; but I say contrary, for in as much as the hawke is exercised by reasonable tyring she becometh the healthier and the lighter both of body and of head by all the moderate exercise, yea, and she is the better in state also as you may perceive". Turbervile 1575

Initial manning will very much depend on whether you yourself took the passage falcon from the wild or if it is one that has been passed on to you. The most important thing to bear in mind is that you need to very carefully formulate your plan of action as regards manning and try where possible to stick to it. You must remember you cannot put the clock back. This may well seem such a blatantly obvious thing to say as to make the author appear stupid, not that I generally need a great deal of help in that direction as a rule. However I have known many falconers that seem to want to rush training and get the falcon on the wing and then set about refining the manning and trying to then, at this late stage, put manners on the falcon. This just isn't going to happen and better to spend slightly longer in initial training and have an extremely well manned falcon than have it on the wing a few days earlier but nervous and suspicious of every little thing and action around it.

A passage falcon comes into the hands of the falconer in an extremely fit and muscled up condition. The falcon has spent several months fending for herself and battling whatever the elements have thrown at her. She is not going to waste away and go to rack and ruin if it takes a week or two longer to get her back on the wing than the training program for an eyass falcon would take. Once the passage falcon is back on the wing, she is proficient and can hunt almost straight away and she will attain her previous level of fitness in no time what so ever. Whereas the eyass falcon should, in capable hands, be on the wing in considerably less time but it will have to be worked quite hard to get any degree of real fitness into it. It certainly will struggle to catch quarry for the first little while unless it is an exceptional falcon or enjoys a few slices of really good luck.

In the case of the passage falcon that was taken by someone else or that has been taken in for whatever reason from the wild to be rehabilitated, you are unlikely to have any say as to how it has been handled up to the point it comes into your possession. I had a passage falcon not so long ago that had been picked up by a farmer and taken to his local vet. The falcon was thin and weak and was probably lucky to have survived a particularly harsh ten days of weather that had affected that part of England at the time. The vet rehydrated the falcon and treated it and then passed it on to a local falconer that supposedly knew what they were doing. Eventually, I was contacted to see if I would take the falcon and try and rehabilitate it. The falconer, in whose hands she now was, remarked how tame she was and how quiet she sat stating that "you would never think she was a wild falcon, she is so well behaved". On receiving the poor unfortunate passager I discovered the reason for her sitting so quiet and being so well behaved. She was acutely thin. The old chestnut about you could use her keel bone to shave with in this case probably was in fact very close to the truth. Prudent and careful feeding gradually put almost six ounces, one hundred and seventy grams, on her and then she looked and most certainly acted completely differently.

Despite the remarks that she was so well behaved and so very quiet and, as I was assured by the supposed falconer, she really won't take much manning as she has been where she can see people and their comings and goings all day, once she was back up to a reasonable weight she was a bitch. She had sat quiet and been tolerant before because she was seriously lethargic due to severe hunger. Once hunger was not an incessant nag and the falcon had time to concentrate on other things than merely trying to stay alive, she decided she didn't really want to tolerate what she saw and was exceedingly free with her bating. Manning sessions were almost self defeating in that she obviously resented being on the fist, tolerating it only to get a meal, and once food was gone she did her best to follow suit. Using tirings considerably extended the time spent on the fist, but it was obvious these were not manning sessions; they were toleration sessions on the part of the falcon. She had to work her way through the tiring to get it replaced by her meal and then once that was over it was time to be anywhere other than on the fist unless hooded, which if care was not taken would merely teach her to resent the hood as it signified the end of a meal. This particular falcon took a great deal of time to be gradually brought round and to become trusting in me and my actions. It came about by plenty of carriage, tirings, bechins and generally being in my company as much as earning my living at the same time would allow. The corrective process with her was a long and often tedious one of repetition and familiarity, but oh so worth all the trouble in the long run. The falcon went on to be an absolute pleasure to be with and handle and would greet my approach with eager anticipation because she had indeed been tamed as well as manned.

From the title of this chapter the reader will have gleaned that I do consider making a wild falcon tame, as well as being well manned, a very important criteria for a successful future partnership between falcon and falconer. Many of my friends in the falconry world disagree with my feelings on the subject and seem to be of the opinion that manning is the process that brings a falcon to a state where she will tolerate man either whole heartedly or, in many cases with passage falcons, somewhat begrudgingly. I truly disagree with this way of looking at things and see the manning and taming process as a two stage operation with quite clear goals in mind for the falconer to strive towards. The first falcon I ever felt like this with, was in actual fact a passage Sakret which came to me from another falconer some forty-four years ago now. The Sakret in question was fiery to say the least and took a considerable while to man down to the stage where he would feed on the fist bareheaded outside in full daylight. However, whenever he was weathered at his block there would be a monumental fight to get him up onto the fist and away from the block, even with a large tit bit of food on the glove or in fact even his entire day's rations. Once up on the fist and a couple of paces away from his block he was fine. It was just the transition from being on his own in what he obviously considered his little piece of territory to coming to my territory and being in my company. That Sakret taught me a great deal about handling passage falcons of any species and the lessons learned have been honed and refined over the years to what is now my more or less standard approach to the manning and taming of any passager. I say more or less with regard to the approach, because there are always occasions when a training regime has to be altered slightly and tailored to an individual that requires it. After all we are discussing living creatures not a set of robotic beings that can be programmed to please and follow set paths without deviation.

However, we shall assume the passage falcon that we are about to discuss the manning and taming of, has come into possession of the falconer in a more normal manner than the one described above. Let me say here that I am very traditional in my thinking when it comes to training and hunting with falcons and although I sometimes try different things that come along, such a kite, quad copters and other such things, it is always out of a sense of curiosity as opposed to a belief that it is a better way to train. I really do believe in the vast majority of cases, particularly when talking of falcons with wild origins, the old tried and tested methods evolved over several hundred years are the best. There is one stage at which I radically disagree with the old teachings however and that is with the early stages of manning. In fact I disagree more or less entirely with the whole process as it used to be carried out and my own experience has taught me that what I do, certainly works for me and for the falcons I train. I most assuredly am not arrogant enough to think that I have a greater wealth of knowledge when it comes to falconry than the old masters whose works I avidly read again and again. It is simply that I do not personally like the traditional method of training a passager and feel that my way arrives at the same ultimate destination but by taking a slightly different route. The end result is that the passager flies quarry well, returns to the falconer without drama when unsuccessful and recalls to the lure as well as weathers at her ease when not working.

For clarification lets quickly look at what was considered the norm when taking up a passage falcon and commencing with her training, of which the first stage is manning which requires her to eat on the fist. The falcon would be carried hooded upon the fist and constantly stroked with a feather to get her used to the indignity of being touched at will by the falconer. After some hours of carriage on the first day of capture or within a short while on the second day if capture was late in the afternoon the previous day, the falcon is induced to eat through the hood by various methods of trickery designed to make the falcon strike at the proffered food out if temper and then be pleasantly surprised when she finds what she is biting at is in fact edible and she quickly tries to quell some of her hunger by taking a number of mouthfuls. This almost enforced feeding will stop and the very slightest of provocations. A movement that is transmitted to her, a sneeze or cough, a door opening, anything that suddenly alters will be enough to terminate that feeding session and to persist will be entirely useless for at least a quite considerable number of hours. For me this

Above: The author with intermewed passage anatum tiercel Mexico. Below left: Author with passage anatum tiercel Mexico. Below right: haggard European tiercel "Tin Tin". This tiercel had been shot and eventually succumbed to his wounds and died.

Above: The last ever passage falcon trapped at Valkenswaard by the Mollens in 1935. The falcon died a couple of days later.

Below left: "Megan" intermewed Eyas Falcon. Below right: "Grace" haggard Falcon.

Above: A relatively unique photograph depicting British Peregrine falcons for intended rehabilitation. Left to right: "Megan" an intermewed eyas. "Gale" an intermewed Falcon Gentle. "Grace" a haggard falcon. "Gillian" a passage falcon.

Below: Diana Durman-Walters and Martin Guzman duck hawking in Mexico with intermewed passage anatum falcon.

Above: Author in Abu Dhabi with intermewed eyas tiercel.

Below left: "Gillian" passage falcon. Below right: Author in Mexico with intermewed passage tundra falcon.

Passage Tundra Peregrines being taken, by means of harnessed pigeons, for research purposes in Mexico.

Above: Stunning example of a passage Tundra peregrine

Below: The Author on a research trip with freshly taken passage Tundra peregrine falcon

scenario is very wrong on two levels. Firstly the falcon is biting and supposedly eventually feeding because it is being provoked to anger. The falcon is in fact being teased into striking out with its beak. Having supposedly become settled enough to be happy to eat what it has been trying to bite, we now reward the falcon for feeding through the hood.

I have to put on record that I passionately do not believe in feeding a falcon through the hood as I believe this teaches them a bad habit that will live with them forever. A falcon that has been taught to feed through the hood, even if only just for a matter of a few days right at the very beginning of her training, will often continue to bite and pull at the glove every time she is on the fist hooded. How is she to know there are times it is perfectly acceptable for her to bend down hooded to try and feed and times when it is not? For me this is a cardinal sin in falconry terms and something I have just never contemplated. If I don't feed, or even attempt to feed, through the hood then it goes without saying I try and get the falcon to eat on the fist, bareheaded, as soon as possible. This is obviously not an easy task, but it is surprising just how quickly a passage falcon will normally take some food from the glove if she is treated with care and furthermore, consideration is given as to how the meal is to be attempted. I am not saying she will take a crop or even anywhere near it but she will, with care and a certain amount of luck, take sustenance levels for two or three days. By the end of that period I am confident that the falcon will feed relatively freely on my fist without being hooded. Having food prepared that the falcon will be happy to eat, such as a quail or pigeon, will help with getting her to feed initially. Also, a pigeon cut in half makes a decent sized piece of food to hold steady in the glove and not have to be repositioned if the falcon starts to feed. Just the motion required to adjust the position of the food on the glove may be sufficient to stop the falcon feeding on the first couple of occasions and having stopped, she is unlikely to start again that day. The careful falconer may well have waited quite literally years to get the opportunity to train and fly a passage falcon and therefore it is reasonable to assume all preparations would have been in place for its arrival and as stated earlier, a plan of action laid down. Not as something to be stuck to no matter, what but certainly to have a set of clearly defined objectives and a reasonable set of progressive steps in mind as to how to reach that goal. Also there should be a clearly defined set of goals that are not to be achieved and trying to feed through the hood, certainly with any falcon I ever have the privilege to fly, is one of them.

Getting back to the old way of doing things, the freshly acquired passager would be induced by the teasing method to feed through the hood for several nights probably nearer a week in actual fact. When she would pull through the hood quite freely, she was subjected to the ritual of being broken to the hood. This was normally carried out at a gathering of friends that would sit around smoking and drinking coffee in a dimly lit room and the falcon would be unhooded and then hooded again quickly and over the course of the evening this process was repeated till she was considered made to the hood. That is when she would allow herself to be hooded without trying to bate from the fist or do an impersonation of a snake, in her attempted avoidance of having the hood put on. Firstly I really dislike the term "broken to the hood" as it implies a bending of the will and battle of force which man will win come what may due to his superior size and strength. No passage or haggard falcon that it has ever been my good fortune to train, has had to be coerced into wearing a hood and in fact with careful use being hooded is actually a state a wild hawk will accept quite readily. Again and again in training the passager shows the falconer that she comes with manners and provided she suffers no ill treatment or heavy handedness on the part of the falconer she will always repay him with her gentle ways that show breeding and class, not traits generally associated with the majority of eyas falcons.

Being able to hood and unhood the falcon without undue drama is an essential stage of training so that other stages can flow gently on from it. Passagers are generally relatively easy to hood for a falconer with the knowledge and patience to do things properly. No need ever to rush getting the hood on and equally never ever under any circumstances cram the hood on or force it down into place with the use of fingers applying pressure to the back of the falcon's head. These are transgressions, no more than that they are indeed sins, that will not be forgotten or forgiven by the falcon and the seed of distrust, which is already laying just under the surface in the mind of the falcon, will probably be germinated into a distrust of the falconer that the passing of time will not heal.

If when acclimatising the passager to wearing the hood she bates from the fist when trying to hood her in the early stages of training, do not panic and consider this the end of the world as we know it. It would be preferable that she didn't bate, but if she does then allow her dignity of regaining the fist and also settling herself comfortably before proffering the hood again. Hooding must not be seen on her part as a negative action in any way shape or form. It is exactly for this reason that when being fed upon the fist the falcon is allowed to finish her meal, pick at bits and pieces on the glove and on her toes, feak if she wishes to, and when all is well with her world she is then hooded. The hood must not come to signal the end of the meal and the production of it must not cause her to think that it is instantly going to be applied. Again, if we look back at the older ways of doing things the hood would be put back on the falcon before she had quite finished her meal and she would then be encouraged to finish her meal through the hood. This was the old way of supposedly teaching a falcon

Phillip Glasier

that indeed the putting on of the hood did not signify the end of the meal. In my mind this action merely taught the falcon to pull at the glove whenever hooded as there was a chance there may well be some food to be had.

When feeding a falcon on the fist in the early days, I always make sure the hood is left in plain sight and if we are walking around then the hood is pinned to my jacket or indeed placed on the little finger of the gloved hand by pushing the little finger through the beak opening of the hood. This is why I constantly harp back to the fact that the falconer themselves must be fully prepared for the training regime they are going to undertake and not suddenly realise part way through a certain stage that some essential ground has not been covered fully. Passagers, in general, are too rare a hawking companion to make unnecessary mistakes with. Think "I will make a note of that fault and ensure it is not repeated next time" is a very poor outlook to take, coupled with the fact that for a great many of us there may not be a next time.

When the passage falcon can be unhooded and then re-hooded without undue drama, it is time to move on with training. Here again my personal training regime differs very greatly from the old, and what is obviously considered, tried and tested way of doing things. The passage falcon of old was hardly unhooded at all during her early weeks of training other than when it was attempted to feed them on the fist. I think this is totally unnecessary and in actual fact can sometimes lead to resentment on the part of the falcon for the falconer and the hood. Problem is, if you put a new passage falcon out to weather that has only just accepted being fed on the fist, without any shadow of doubt she is going to bate more or less constantly. This will have the two fold effect of creating severe frustration within the mind of the falcon and also will most definitely lead to the damage of train feathers and primaries. Hence something of a dilemma for the falconer who cares about the mental as well as physical state of the falcon but still wants to man her and eventually tame her. Anyone can man a falcon, but taming, which in my mind is truly essential, is a different thing. A falcon that is induced to tolerate the presence of man and all his accompaniments through appetite and restrictive practices is not likely to become tame. My own belief is that you can truly tame a wild falcon to the point where it enjoys your company and will, on occasions, seek you out. I have had a passage Saker Falcon chase rooks over the horizon before the days of telemetry and that very Saker has come back some twenty minutes later and perched on a branch of tree above my head. She then jumped down to the fist with no food being proffered. That is what I mean by being tame. She literally sought me out and it wasn't the ever present spark of appetite that drove her to do so.

My way of dealing with the weathering dilemma is to use high perches right from the word go. Let me make it perfectly clear that I mean what are known as high perches and most certainly not high blocks. For those that are unaware of the difference, a high block is precisely that, in that it is a conventional block other than the fact the stem between the ground and the block itself is two or three and sometimes even four foot in length and accordingly lifts the actual block that much above the ground. The falcon is still tethered leash length to a ring that encircles the spike of the block. Should the falcon bate off of the block it will end up on the ground just its own leash length away from the spike. It then has to pump quite hard to regain the height of the block because of the relatively acute angle. Those that favour these types of block don't generally use them with passage falcons, eyas falcons would be the normal order of the day, and also they tend to be used with falcons that are already being flown in earnest. Those that use them say that falcons seem to prefer sitting higher and are therefore less restless when being weathered.

The high perch is a cylindrical plastic tube with a capped top that is some three to four feet high and has a base of sufficient dimension as to provide stability when in use. The top and first foot going down from the top towards the base of the tube are covered in astro-turf and a hole of sufficient diameter to pass the leash through is drilled centrally on the top most surface of the perch which is itself around eight inches in diameter. About one foot down the tube from the top two holes are drilled one slightly above the other. The top hole is approximately one inch in diameter and is used to pass the leash through when securing the falcon to the perch. The second hole is some four inches in diameter and means the falconer can, if needs be, get his fist inside the tube. The Falcon is secured to this type of perch by passing the leash through the hole in the centre top plate, until the swivel is stopping the leash from actually going any further, and then pulling out through the larger lower hole. The leash is then passed through the small hole and back out of the large one again and then this is repeated again till finally the end of the leash is passed beneath the three strands of leash that go from lower hole to top hole and then the leash is pulled tight and for safety's sake repeated again. The falcon cannot possible get the leash out or undone. For added stability on my high perches I have a two foot diameter circular plate made of plastic on the bottom of the tube as well which means I can fill the tube with water and this increase in weight provides excellent stability. These high perches have transformed how I set about manning and taming passage falcons. They are a relatively recent piece of equipment to come onto the market and as soon as I saw the potential in the early days, it must be said somewhat crude versions that were offered for sale, I drew up an improved design and got half a dozen made up to my own specifications. One of the best things I ever did with regards to equipment.

Now instead of weathering a falcon for several weeks hooded with her only having the hood off to feed or when placed in a completely light tight mews my passager comes out on day two or three to weather. Admittedly for the first hour or so the falcon is hooded and then the braces of the hood are struck and after a few moments removed. It goes without saying that the falcon will bate but because her swivel is pulled up hard to the central plate of the perch she can only bate the length of her jesses. At first she will bate at more or less any provocation but this should have been taken into consideration by the falconer and her tail will have been taped up with old fashioned gummed paper, the type you wet to make sticky and then wet again heavily to remove. Also the falcon would have been put out close to the time she would have been fed on the fist. It is at this moment that training, manning and taming should all move forward coherently. Bechins will have been prepared and each time the falconer passes the falcon he will speak to her and give her a bechin which she will almost certainly refuse. So just put it on the perch in front of her and move on. Few minutes later come back past, speaking softly as you do, and proffer another bechin, again she almost assuredly won't take it directly but leave it on the perch in front of her. She will eat it the moment you are either a fair distance away or are out of sight. This process is repeated over and over till around one third of the intended meal for the falcon has been consumed.

When I first adopted this approach I used to place the high perch in the quietest spot I could find and try and leave the passage falcon in as much peace as possible. I soon realised this was exactly the opposite of what I should be doing, relative to my own circumstances. I now place the high perch where dogs can pass by; the falcon can see into the house through a window and can hear things in the street just over the wall. When the perch was placed somewhere quiet each and every new experience was treated with dread and became a major stepping stone. With having the perch now in the close proximity of the sorts of things the falcon will see in her everyday home life when she is trained we seem to get past the "my god what on earth is this new horror" stage within a couple of days. It is literally amazing how quickly a passage falcon will sit on one of these high perches, with one foot tucked up, feathers slightly fluffed out and look down quite unconcernedly on several dogs running round her.

Not many of the old works on falconry make much of the falconer talking to his hawks but I believe this really is an essential part of the manning process. A raised voice is most definitely a negative thing and why I don't for one millionth of a second think a bird of prey can understand what we are saying a raised voice must mean something different to them than the constant quieter tones they have come to expect from their future hunting partner. Also presumably a raised voice would normally accompany actions which are jerkier and more violent in their execution. It is easy to say but it really is essential that you do not lose your temper or even let yourself get above your regular calm and focused self when dealing with a falcon. No matter what the irritation the falconer may be subjected to, calmness and regularity in your handling of the falcon and your responses to her must be the order of the day. Just as a dog has no real idea what we are saying to it the tone and volume of our voice is what the communication is judged on. How easy is it to calm an agitated dog by gently talking to it, I would say surprisingly so. For me a falcon responds well to a soft voice that is well known to it, it is a reassurance and a constant to be relied upon. It has often been remarked that patience is one of the absolutely key elements required by a falconer when it comes to training hawks. The point is stressed again and again in various works on the subject. Those that know me well will be fully aware of the fact I personally have very little patience, but my plus point is that I am completely aware of the fact and acknowledge it. Accordingly when training a falcon if I reach a point where my limited patience is being stretched, I cease what I am doing as quickly as is feasibly possible and put the falcon down and take a break until serenity is restored within me.

Having reached the stage with our passager where she will accept bechins when weathering on her high perch, allow me to pick her up from it without too much drama and then feed relatively freely on the fist. It is time to move on. The next step is to walk round with the falcon on the fist whilst she feeds. However falcons can put a day's food ration away pretty quickly and therefore the training time, unless artificially elongated, will be a relatively short one. The meal can be considerably prolonged with the use of decent tirings. As with so much of modern falconry it is unfortunate that tirings, along with rangle and bechins, seem to be relegated to some form of mental falconry museum. Tirings are a very useful tool in the falconer's arsenal and serve several purposes as well as prolonging a meal and therefore prolonging the training time in these relatively early stages of the working partnership between falcon and falconer. When falcons are being moulted at the block tirings, especially very meagre ones, will keep a falcon occupied for a considerable time as well as exercise many muscles that would normally otherwise get little use at this time of general idleness. The constant picking and pulling at the tiring and the effort expended in holding it down so as to be able to get at it all mean work for various muscles. At the end of the session with a tiring, the falcon has actually gained very little food from the exercise but her mind, as well as her body have been occupied.

When using a tiring for prolonging a falcons meal in the training stages I would suggest that slightly more meat than is normal is left on what it is that is being used. Probably one of the best to use is the front leg of a rabbit with the vast majority of the meat removed. Often recommended as a suitable tiring is the backbone of a rabbit, however I have found on two occasions that falcons have split their beaks on such a tiring and consequently never use them. A pigeon wing or a duck wing also make excellent tirings but they tend to be discarded relatively quickly due to the visible meat being quite easy to actually get to. Chicken and duck necks also make first class tirings ideally suited to the job. They appear to be just one big lump of meat but in actual fact contain very little meat and the meat that is present is not easy to remove. Such tirings will keep a falcon occupied for a considerable time. When it gets to the stage that the falconer wants to move on and feed the falcon on the fist, or perhaps start to initiate jumping to the fist then it is a simple matter to remove the tiring from the fist without the falcon feeling it has been robbed.

Both tirings and bechins are not items merely to be employed when a falcon is being trained. Tirings have their uses as already stated and also when flying on certain days is not just possible and the falconer doesn't want the contact with the falcon to be a brief session lasting only as long as it takes the falcon to feed. Bechins should be given to the falcon for the rest of her life that she chooses to spend with the falconer. Obviously not in the copious quantities that were used in the early days but the effect of giving an unsolicited tit bit to a falcon will never ever be considered with a negative thought on her part. The use of bechins at all stages and in all circumstances help builds a bond between falcon and falconer. From the falcon's point of view the bechin is a treat and a very positive action from the person she has chosen to work with. I remember on one occasion a display falconer exercising a tiercel that repeatedly landed at his feet and would not actually fly off at all. He marked how well bonded the tiercel was to him and how loyal he was being. Of course the truth was the tiercel was desperately hungry and being flown on hunger and appetite alone. The saying that "There are none so blind as those that won't see" sprung to mind.

I make sure that throughout the early lessons, particularly when the falcon is actually occupied with feeding on the fist, that I make a point of touching her petty singles as well as her lower leg. I want that later in life switching from mews to flying jesses, or removing bullet jess system is a painless operation for both of us. Also I don't want to be picking detritus from her feet or greasing an anklet as she sits on the fist to be a negative experience for her. This is why I stress that even before the start of the onset of training the falconer needs to have clearly defined goals he needs to achieve and a plan by which they are ticked off one by one. The early days of training are, for me in my mind, where the real pleasure of being in a particular falcon's company in the future is won or lost. Hasty training and a giving in to peer pressure to complete training in the shortest possible time pays dividends of a very unpleasant sort for the rest of the duration of the working partnership. Time in the early days spent encouraging the natural good manners of the falcon will repay itself a hundred fold.

A good example of this is the use of the high perch, of which I never get tired of praising the virtues of. It has radically changed how I train all falcons in general and passage falcons in particular. All falconers are aware that if you put a freshly trapped passage falcon out to weather bareheaded within two or three days of being taken, it will spend its entire time bating in a burning desire to be somewhere else. This trait will then continue to the same or perhaps just slightly lesser degree ad infinitum. I well remember an occasion when I was in the States and talking to a falconer with a passage Tundra Peregrine that was doing its best to dig a trench in the ground around its block by constantly bating. The efforts of this falcon to be somewhere else were exceedingly strenuous and certainly relentless. The falconer was stood close by as it pained him to see her acting so, but the only time she stopped was when on the fist or hooded. Even when he sat on the ground close to her and spoke gently the falcon persisted in its escape efforts. We spoke about the cause of this behaviour and it transpired the falcon had been put out to weather bareheaded within a week of being taken. I am afraid to say this falcon consequently never settled and every flight was an occasion to be on tenterhooks. If she killed, she was very difficult to approach and required the falconer to cover the last five to ten yards to her on his stomach. If she failed to kill it would require a track down as she would look for something else and when found, would be hesitant at coming in to the lure and then as equally difficult to pick up from it as it would have been from a kill. Needless to say this partnership did not last long with the falcon eventually parting company with the falconer. Just as an aside, my falconer friends in Mexico that fly passage falcons do so without telemetry in their first season together. They say the odds of losing the passager in her first season are around fifty-fifty so if she is likely to be lost, then why lose an expensive transmitter as well.

Passager on the first

With the use of the high perch this trait is eradicated and eventually being put out to weather on a conventional block will be perfectly acceptable to the passager and she will not spend her entire time bating. There does have to be a transition to a conventional block, if only two or three times a week, so as to enable the falcon to be offered a bath. To deprive any falcon of the opportunity to bathe on a regular basis is incredibly poor husbandry. To do so with a Peregrine falcon of any description is nothing less than deliberate cruelty. Peregrines love to bathe, whether it be a quick in and out or a total immersion and thorough soaking. Either way the choice to do so or not, should be theirs.

Again a falcon that has regained the block having just indulged in a bath would be sure to appreciate the approach of the falconer offering a bechin. Many opportunities will present themselves in the day to day home life of the falcon where bechins will prove a useful tool in forging a thoroughly trusting regard for the falconer within the mind of the falcon. Take advantage of these moments to cement a good relationship. Carriage, even though the falcon is hooded, is a good thing provided it is before the main meal of the day has been given along with any training that accompanies it. I feel that once a training session is over the falcon needs to be put away and left to her own devices. I believe that to carry on with carriage would probably serve as an irritant. I am talking now of the first two to three weeks of training not in later life when the falcon is flying and hunting. Spending as much time as you can with the passage falcon in the early days of your relationship together is very important. That is of course provided the time spent is of a positive nature. From the point of view of the falcon then, a lot of the early time will not be what she would consider pleasant or in the least desirable. She is being made to spend time in the close proximity of man and also has something of a nagging hunger that persists certainly for the first few days. However with carriage, food, kindness, soft voice and gentle actions the falcon will be won round and not only tolerate her partner but with care will eventually get to be content to spend time in his or her company. That should be the aim of the falconer from the moment the passager is removed from the net or harness and comes, with an unblemished record, into his possession.

Let me end with one final thought that will instil absolute horror in a true traditionalist and may seem close to falconry blasphemy. In the first two or three days that the passage falcon is in the possession of the falconer I am not a believer that the falcon should not feed until it does so on the fist. I am also not a believer in starving a falcon into submission even at this critically early stage. So although it may seem like an absolute sin against the laws of falconry I let the falcon have a small amount of food, certainly for the first three days or so, if it won't feed at all on the fist. This is easy to engineer in that a gutted chick is placed on top of the high perch when the falcon has bated off or if she is surprisingly steady then a gloved hand can be placed palm downwards on the top of the high perch and the small amount of food deposited beneath it and when the hand is drawn away then the food is revealed. The falconer can then walk away so as not to be directly associated with depositing the food. Otherwise this would encourage the falcon to be resolutely stubborn as she would soon learn she is to be fed even if she chooses not to do so on the fist.

The fact that the passager was taken means she was ready to eat and to then allow her to shut down her system for a few days is certainly harmful and most definitely not desirable. I would far rather training took a day or two longer but with a falcon that was enjoying full health. Her system will already be under strain from the whole capture and initiation of training process without adding to her troubles. A good falconer will strive to ensure the health and happiness of his falcon as well as her prowess in the field. If this is not the attitude that is readily adopted, then perhaps another sport, not involving working with living creatures, should be considered.

Passage falcons are pearls beyond price. Enjoy every second that they are with you. For a falconer there can be no better experience than training and then hunting with a passage falcon.

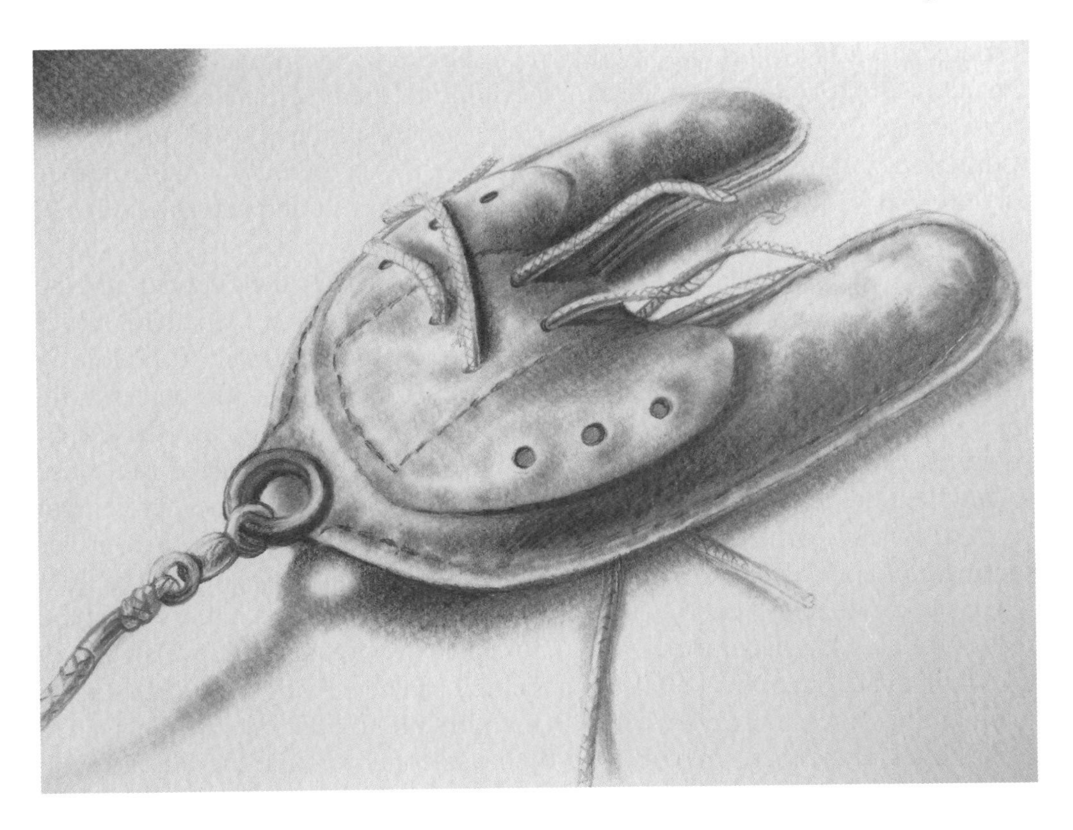

THE LURE, INTRODUCTION AND CALLING OFF

The lure is an absolutely essential piece of equipment that arguably cannot be done without for those that wish to train and hunt falcons. I say arguably because there are a small number of falconers on the North American continent that are experimenting with training large falcons to the glove only. I have only seen two falcons flown in such a manner and neither was any more or any less successful at quarry than a conventionally lure trained falcon. However, on the occasions I went out with them, their obedience to the fist was at times erratic. This may well have been that the principle is actually a good one but the practical side of things with these two particular falcons had not been reinforced sufficiently. To me the experiment was purely that. I failed to see why not introducing a falcon to the lure and having the fist only as a recall method was in any way advantageous to the tried and trusted traditional lure method. Not to mention the fact that you can hardly stoop a falcon to the fist to increase fitness and build muscle. Nor was any serious reason for the experiment offered other than purely to see what would happen. Whilst

I appreciate it is all too easy to become a blinkered traditionalist and not be prepared to encompass new ideas, or even give them serious consideration, there is also the argument that if something works extremely well and serves its intended purpose superbly then why change it. Accordingly in this instance the lure and its use in educating the falcon, getting it fit and acting as a recall method will be taken as the norm.

The lure and its application serve several purposes for the falconer and the falcon that is being trained to think of it as a food source. It should never be forgotten at any point that falcon and falconer tend to think of the lure in different ways. From the falconer's point of view once a falcon has successfully been introduced to the lure, training can progress quite rapidly and the falcon should be on the wing, flying free, relatively soon. In the case of the eyass falcon then the lure can be used to give her muscle tone and raise her general level of fitness. When she is flying the lure with a degree of gusto then her footing ability should also increase. This will pay dividends later in the field when she is pursuing quarry in earnest. With a passage falcon, unless for some reason training has become protracted, to regain previous fitness levels will not take long at all. Exercising a falcon to the lure can be employed as a method of maintaining fitness on days when it is not possible to hunt quarry. Finally the lure is a recall mechanism employed by the falconer to quite literally lure the falcon back after an unsuccessful flight at quarry. What should never ever be forgotten is that the partnership between passage falcon and falconer is, to say the least, a very tenuous one and, as with every aspect of falconry, great care must be taken when making into a passage falcon on the lure and taking her up from it. Never make the mistake of initiating any short cuts when taking the falcon up due to her supposed familiarity with the process, a habit that can all too easily be slipped into when dealing with eyass falcons. The slightest thing can turn a docile and obedient passage falcon that dropped out of the sky to the proffered lure instantaneously, to an almost wild untrusting hawk that will actually step off of the lure at the approach of the falconer. Something I would have had trouble believing had I not witnessed it myself. On this occasion the falconer didn't want to kneel down on wet grass to take up the falcon and so bent over her to proffer the fist. The falcon stepped back, weighed up the situation and then took to the wing never to be recovered. The action was out of her routine, made her feel threatened by the falconer towering over her and the obvious way to deal with it, from her point of view, was to be elsewhere.

From the point of view of the falcon, the lure offers a relatively easy option to obtain a small food reward which can, on most occasions, lead to an easy meal on the fist of the falconer. Therefore, if the falcon was introduced to the lure correctly, has never been robbed whilst on it or carelessly and hurriedly taken up from it, it will always serve as an exceedingly effective recall trigger. Food must be attached with considerable care as under no circumstances should it be capable of coming off the lure when the lure is being swung or be capable of being pulled off by the falcon when she has come down to it. If the falcon finds herself sitting on the ground with a larger than normal tit bit she will either eat it quickly and look to the glove for more or, as is often the case, bolt off with the food with the intention of getting up somewhere higher to eat it. I myself have made the cardinal error at the next stage of the proceedings which is probably worth mentioning at this juncture.

I had a haggard falcon come into the lure on what was a particularly blustery day. This falcon was always a little nervous on the lure and it was my habit to sit away from her a few feet and let her eat the tit bit from the lure then she would take a couple of steps closer to me and then jump up to the fist. On the day in question, the falcon was being buffeted by the wind as she sat on the lure and having finished the food on it was acting a little hesitantly with regard to coming to the fist. I proffered her on the glove a quail, which had been gutted and had had the wings and feet removed. She finally jumped to the fist and in one swift movement snatched the quail and made off several yards to a post with her prize. I was fully aware that to immediately try and go to her to take her up would result in her taking wing so I sat where I was, talking to her all

Tiercel on lure

the time, and waiting for her to get well and truly engrossed in her meal. When she was well into her meal I approached slowly and talking to her proffered the fist with some more food on it. Needless to say I got to within a couple of feet of her before she spread her wings and let the wind take her to a tree some distance away. I was still fairly calm, as this was quite a greedy falcon when it came to feed and I hoped that between her finishing her quail and actually starting to put it over I stood quite a good chance of her coming down to the lure. After all just because food is in the crop it does not mean the appetite of the falcon has been sated.

Accordingly I waited for her to finish her illicit meal and as soon as I saw her start to feak, I proffered the lure again at a distance sufficiently far from the tree that she could simply glide down directly into the wind; so the opportunity to stop should have outweighed the temptation to over shoot and carry on. However the best laid plans of mice and men don't always work out and she did indeed sail on past and it was another thirty hours before she was safely back on the fist again. I had initially made a very basic error by not having sufficient grip on the food I had offered on the glove and most certainly was made to think long and hard about the mistake as I tracked her for the rest of that day and part of the next before finally being re-united with her.

The normal lure consists of a stuffed leather horseshoe shaped pad which will vary in size and weight, depending on the species of falcon for which it is intended. Strings will protrude in the centre of the pad on each side for the attachment of the food reward. The pad will then be connected to a swivel, which is in turn connected to a cotton line of some five yards and the other end of this line is attached to a lure stick. The function of the swivel is to ensure that the line does not become twisted when the lure is swung. Using cotton line means there is no friction burn to the falconer if the lure line is pulled quickly through the hand, such as when stooping a falcon to the lure. Strings protrude from both sides so that the meat attached to the pad can clearly be seen whichever way up the lure is presented to the falcon, or if it is thrown out on the ground. The stick is dual purpose in that it is a convenient place to wrap the lure line around when the lure is not in use and can also act as a drag should a nervous or bolshie falcon try and make off with the lure when approached. Designs for the main body of the lure can vary greatly from one falconer to another and everyone has their own idea as to what makes the perfect lure. Whatever design is settled upon by the individual falconer it should be borne in mind a lot of falcons don't accept change readily, so when I make a lure for a new falcon I always make two pretty much the same. Hence if something happens to my regular lure I have an almost identical back up to hand if required.

A lure is meant to represent a bird to the falcon and some falconers do go to extra ordinary lengths to try and make the lure seem lifelike. Wings of the quarry species to be flown are attached and some even go so far as to paint the body of the lure to resemble a bird. All of which I think rather underestimates the intelligence of the falcon. I cannot really believe that any falconer can truly think that a Peregrine Falcon will think that a leather pad with some Rook wings attached being swung in a totally unnatural way will suddenly lead her to think she has indeed spied a Rook. What the falcon will do, if it has been conditioned correctly, is realise that the production of the lure could very well mean a meal is in the offing and therefore it will hurry over to investigate the possibility. Some would argue that if a falcon intended for Rook hawking is exercised to a lure that has black wings attached it will help her when it comes to hunting them. When she has reached the stage of being ready to enter and is unhooded and cast off at a group of Rooks the black wings will act as stimuli and she will think of them as food. Personally I doubt this very much. What I prefer to do with a hawk intended for Rooks is exercise her and muscle her up on a lure pad without wings but call her down at the end of the lesson to a dead Rook.

A great many years ago when my practical day to day experience was considerably less and I slavishly followed the contemporary falconry books of the time I did dress my lures with wings. The whole process was a tedious one as the falcon would inevitably end up plucking at the wings and they would have to be renewed on a regular basis. Eventually I became tired of this and decided just to use lures which consisted of a plain leather pad without any adornment. What matters far more than any artificial dressing up is that the falcon comes to learn that the production of the lure means she is going to get a meal very shortly. She may have to chase it for a while first, but it does signify a meal is in the offing. The only exception to my own rule about not putting wings on a lure is in the case of any falcon I flew at grouse. As grouse moors tend to have a consistently dark background, I have used Mallard wings on my lures for my grouse hawks. I have always felt that the flash of white in the wings of the duck may possibly help the falcon spot the lure somewhat easier than if there were no wings on it. But having said that the last Jerkin and Barbary Falcon that I flew on the moors were flown to a lure that had no wings on it and they never seemed to have any difficulty spotting it when it was being swung. So I shall now probably abandon the use of wings altogether other than with very small falcons such as Aplomado, Hobby, Merlin, American Kestrel and the like. With these species I still tend to use a couple of pairs of fresh Quail wings cable tied together and use this as the body or the lure itself. Then a small garnish can be added at you have a light simple and effective lure. The small falcons pull at the wings and I can tit bit them whilst they are on the lure and then take them up with a suitable piece of food. This tit biting whilst on the lure really is so very vital, especially with any species that has a reputation for carrying, such as Merlin or Hobby. It is a means of teaching the falcon to trust you and your approach to feel safe whilst on the lure and that sitting on it will always lead to good things, ie food.

When a falcon is being trained initially, the introduction to the lure should be a straight forward process. If you intend to fly your falcon over dogs then make sure a dog is present at all times, not only during these lessons but right from day one. You will be amazed how quickly the falcon accepts the presence of the dog at this stage, that is whilst simply everything is new and to a certain degree frightening to the falcon. Much better to introduce the dogs now along with all the other things it is going to have to get used to, than when the falcon is already flying loose and can clear off if it is feeling threatened. Introduction to the lure will directly follow on from the falcon being called to the fist. I have never been happy calling any falcon of mine too far to the fist in the early days and generally speaking as soon as the falcon moves from jumping the length of its leash to a matter of two or three metres on the creance, then the lure becomes the recall mechanism used from that point forward. Obviously it makes sense to jump the falcon to the fist occasionally just as a reminder, but this really does have to be nothing more than a once in a blue moon exercise. For the first couple of lessons I kneel down beside the block and jump the falcon to the fist a couple of times to get her interested in her meal. I then remove the leash and swivel and attach the creance to the slits of the mews jesses by means of a falconers knot. I never ever use a creance that has any form of spring clip fitted to the end of it, nor do I attach the creance to the swivel. In my opinion both these practices are dangerous and have impending accident written all over them. I prefer that the weakest link in the set up, when a falcon is on the creance, to be the leather of the jesses. If any part is to fail, it is much better it be the leather. In this way the falcon does not go off with its legs handcuffed together.

With the falcon settled on the fist I throw out a well garnished lure on the ground just a couple of feet in front of her and at the same time blow the whistle I would have been using to call her with. By well garnished, I mean precisely that. You cannot expect a fresh falcon that is being asked to do something alien to it for a food reward, to do this willingly, when the food reward is hardly worth having. For a large falcon I cut a breast of quail in such a fashion that there is a decent chunk of meat still attached to the wing. In this way there is a food the falcon will like but it cannot be greedily gobbled down in a couple of bites. It has to be pulled at and whilst this pulling takes place bechins can be introduced. For a small falcon I normally use a quail leg with just the bottom foot part cut off. Again it is a particular food the falcon will like but will take considerable time to consume. These early lessons are vitally important and will set the tone for your hunting collaboration with this falcon for many years to come. Most falcons, as strange as it may seem, will not hop down immediately. Instead they will ponder the lure from every possible angle and lean forward as if to drop on it but at the last minute settle back on the fist. Very similar to the way that most eyass falcons are reluctant to take that first initial jump to the fist. The will to commit themselves completely seems to be somewhat lacking. Quite a number may well need to be lowered a little towards the lure. At this stage some falcons will hop directly onto the lure, others will land beside it and then foot the lure before getting on it.

Don't be tempted to rush and try and force the issue, almost inevitably the falcon will end up on the lure. The important thing now is to make sure the falcon does not feel under threat and eats the food from the lure where it is and doesn't make any attempt to carry the lure off somewhere else. I make sure I position myself between the falcon and her block as this is a convenient and trusted perch she may well be tempted to try and carry the lure to. I also run my hand down the lure line and ensure that the lure is grasped securely to forestall any idea of it being carried. Then with the other hand I offer tit bits to the falcon and help and encourage her to feed from the lure. This lesson can be repeated in each training session but unless things go wrong my own policy is to only call a falcon to the lure once. Right from day one, I want the lure to signify a meal is in the offing and that to return to it when asked to do so will always be a worthwhile proposition.

I cannot stress too highly the need to eradicate any thoughts the falcon may have with regard to carrying the lure. This is a passage falcon we are discussing and therefore a falcon that has killed many times for herself and also chosen equally as many times as to where she would prefer to eat her meal and feel safe in doing so. Her natural inclination will be to carry her meal off to somewhere she considers suitable to her needs and away from any possible danger. Ergo her natural instinct is to carry and is only a vice as far as the falconer is concerned, not the falcon. The need to eat at the very spot the meal is proffered is a trait that needs to be very carefully installed in the mind of the falcon by the falconer and the natural instinct to select an alternative on the part of the falcon overcome. Accordingly, ensure this part of the re-education of the falcon is taken at a pace she is comfortable with and not rushed in any way. If this stage of the training does not go right and the falcon still retains the desire to select her own place to take her meal, then the somewhat tenuous hold the falconer has over his or her passager will be weakened considerably. Sooner, rather than later, the passager will be lost as a result.

After two or three days the falcon will alight on the lure the instant it is shown and will eat contentedly from it. In these early days it is advisable to put a large garnish on the lure and one that is quite bony and requires the falcon to pick at it a great deal in order to get her meal. Whilst she is engaged in eating you can give her a bechin or two, then walk slowly around her and approach from a different angle. Give her another bechin or two and repeat the process. You want the falcon to accept you whilst she is on the lure and not to be panicked by your approach. I must admit with every new falcon I train this point in its education always leaves me in somewhat of a quandary. Just how far do you take things at this juncture? I like it that generally speaking I can approach my falcon on either the lure or a kill and offer them bechins without them being the least bit worried at my presence. My current falcon will stop feeding on the lure or kill as I kneel down beside her and await the bechins she knows will surely materialise. However, I am always nervous at the thought of a lost falcon feeding on a kill somewhere and being happy and contented as well as completely trusting whilst being approached by someone who very well may intend her harm. It is a difficult question to answer. These lessons should end with the falcon being encouraged to jump or step back up onto the fist for a decent reward. So make sure she has not eaten her fill on the lure and that the food on your glove is just as tasty a proposition to her as that which was on the lure.

Sakret about to take the lure

Once this stage has been reached then the process of calling the falcon off on the creance longer and longer distances to the lure can begin. This can be achieved by the falconer on his or her own, but is so much easier with the help of an extra pair of hands. The falcon is left hooded on the fist of an assistant as the falconer moves away a few yards. If there is any breeze at all then this will be directly into the wind so as to aid the falcon with takeoff and landing. The falcon has the braces of the hood struck and then after several moments the hood is removed. Never strike the braces and then whip the hood straight off all in one movement. A falcon will very soon get to where it is highly agitated the minute it feels you taking hold of the hood braces. It is a lesson once learnt that is almost impossible to correct. If it does pick up this vice then it will be troublesome to both hood and unhood in the future. If you are game hawking there is absolutely no need what so ever to get the falcon into the air within a few seconds so consequently there is no need to get the hood off quickly. If you are hawking quarry out of the hood, then no slip should ever take the falconer utterly by surprise. Therefore when a potential slip is spotted, the braces can be struck. If a flight does ensue then the hood can be removed. If it is a false alarm then the braces can be done up again. Either way, just as with everything else to do with falconry, the unhooding of the falcon should be a very calm, considered and measured action.

The first thing the falcon should see on the removal of the hood is the lure being swung and then dropped on the ground just a short distance away. She will also hear the whistle that the falconer will blow to accompany the lure being swung. Practically every time this scenario will result in the falcon acting like a large butterfly and gently landing on the lure. Very occasionally, a new falcon will power towards the lure and inevitably over shoot it. If it does so, then it will be pulled up by the creance and the lure can be swung and dropped out for it again. More often than not in such a case a falcon will run over to the lure, with the ridiculous gait that all falcons have, and then alight on it. If the falcon does seem a little confused and unsure what to do next, then walk round in front of her and drop the lure close by, giving a blast on the whistle. Try and ensure at all costs that she doesn't think this is a fruitless exercise and try and fly off. Drop the lure practically at her feet, if this is what you think at the time it will take to keep her interested. If the falcon then steps on the lure and eats give her plenty of encouragement by breaking bits of food off for her and giving them to her with your fingers. Never, ever, be rushed in any aspect of training and don't let yourself be governed by what you believe others may think. When I was younger I used to have a self imposed timetable in my head as to what progress should be made and at what rate. It would worry me if I thought a stage of training was taking too long. Now I am the exact opposite. I would rather take considerably longer and get the training absolutely right than have to live with the consequences of rushing things. I have flown some of my falcons for more than twenty years so what possible point is there in trying to get one into the air a few days earlier than sensible training would dictate.

Once progress has been made beyond fifteen feet or so, the lure should be swung when the falcon is called. Each day the distance the falcon is called off can be increased until she is coming eighty to a hundred yards. But what is far more important than distance is the promptness of the falcon's reaction. Having a falcon that will come a hundred yards but only after having thought about it for several minutes is not what you are after. As soon as the falcon catches sight of the lure she should be on her way to it. What is important at this stage is that the falcon should come to a swung lure and not just one that is simply thrown out. Throwing the lure out onto the ground immediately is only for the first few basic introduction lessons and as a recall signal if all else fails. Once the falcon is being called any distance she should be called to a swung lure which is accompanied by a few short blasts on the whistle. She will only ever be called to a lure dropped onto the ground when she is going to be given it. She must learn that a lure on the ground is hers and is not going to be whipped up and swung again when she has responded to it and is on her way.

I carry out two further little exercises before I fly my falcons loose after this basic lure training. The first is to see if they will take the lure in the air. This I bring about by swinging the lure until the falcon is about three quarters of the way to me and then I stop swinging and dangle the lure a foot or so off of the ground. I have never had a falcon yet not take the lure from this position but better safe than sorry. Better to find out if there is a problem or not whilst the falcon is still on the creance. The other safety check is to make sure the falcon will turn if you whip the lure behind your back and out of the way as she makes her final approach. If she looks back at you as she goes past, then blow the whistle and throw the lure out immediately. If she comes back round to it then all is well and she can go loose. What may well happen is that instead of looking back as she continues to fly the falcon will land on the ground in front of you or momentarily hovers above you looking for the lure. In either case sprint off a little way and blow the whistle and throw the lure out. Just repeat the procedure the next day and the next if required. Sooner or later the falcon will get the idea.

Once she will take the lure in the air and will turn when it is whipped away she is ready to be flown loose. Now stooping lessons can begin in earnest and day by day she will become fitter. All books always make the remark that you will now make rapid progress from this point on. However what if your falcon instead of making passes at the lure either flutters to the ground in apparent confusion as to what is required of it or, far worse, just carries on flying when you whip the lure away and tries to disappear into the distance. Most books don't mention this and it is all too easy to think that you are the only person it has ever happened to. Of the two faults the second is the easiest to fix. If the falcon carries on without looking back then I am afraid it needs to be a little sharper and or a little more focused on the lure. Don't be afraid of going backwards a few days and reinforcing the introduction to the lure and strengthening the bond between the falcon and the impending meal it almost inevitably means in these early days. The fluttering to the ground and looking up at the falconer in total bewilderment is something that would normally happen with an eyass but I have had it happen with a haggard and indeed my last passage falcon.

Should the falcon land on the ground close by, instantly hide the lure and run off directly into the wind and do not attempt to call the falcon again till you are at least eighty to a hundred yards away. If this fails and she follows you and lands again on no account throw the lure out. Rather proffer the fist and take her up on it. Hood her up and after a short break try her again. If still no joy, I once had a passage Lugger Falcon that took twelve days to learn the simple task of making a pass at the lure, then again take her up on the fist without throwing the lure down beside her and try her again the following day. What finally got the Lugger Falcon going for me was that I did just about everything you are not supposed to do when training a falcon. I found a good sized hill with the wind blowing directly down it. I got a friend to stand on top with the falcon and then I went to the bottom and lured the falcon to me. She came down hill and with a stiff wind blowing her along. She arrived at the lure with such speed that when it was whipped away she had no choice other than to turn round as the wind was pushing her hard and just landing at my feet would have been more difficult than turning and coming into the lure. Of course when she turned she was then flying into the wind and so was lifted a little and made the whole job very easy for her. I know the method is very unconventional but it has also worked with a captive bred Saker Falcon that was also initially reluctant to turn and chase a lure.

As soon as she can put in twenty good passes without being out of breath then she is ready to go hawking. This is the same stage at which you would be looking to enter an eyass but of course the passager has killed for herself a great many times before. A falcon needs to be fit and truly muscled up before she can be expected to fly quarry with any reasonable chance of success. Whenever I stoop one of my falcons to the lure and I decide that the exercise has come to an end and I am going to give the lure to her I shout "Ho" and either throw the lure on the ground or deliberately let her catch me out on the next pass. Either way, the thing to remember is never under any circumstance ever cheat your falcon. If you do, she will remember it forever and you would have undone a great deal of the trust she has willingly placed in you. If you give the shout for her to have the lure then you must give it to her. If she plays you up one day and is loitering down wind or is just generally reluctant to come in do not shout

"Ho" and throw the lure out only to whip it away again when she responds to it. If you do you will pay dearly for the deception sooner or later.

Once a falcon is truly fit and flying well to the lure, attacking it with gusto, be careful as to how you let her take it at the end of the exercise period. Some people throw the lure up high into the air and the falcon powers up and takes it. This may well look spectacular in bird of prey displays at centres and country fairs, but no quarry species I have come across would ever act like this and there is also a very real danger the lure line could wrap itself around the wing of the falcon. I have seen it happen more than once. It must be said that the only people I have seen end luring sessions with such dramatic actions are those that fly falcons in bird of prey displays and not those that actually hunt with falcons. The two disciplines are simply poles apart and bear little realistic comparison to each other. I think far more of my falcons than to risk a potentially serious injury by performing a circus trick with them. Better to lead the falcon through on a pass and slow your swing down just sufficiently for her to take it. If in any doubt then let her make a down wind pass, then shout and throw the lure out on the ground. She will turn and land on it but most of the speed she has gained will have been lost.

When giving initial calling off lessons there may well be occasions when the falconer finds himself without someone to assist. Therefore he has no one to remove the hood from the falcon and also to wait before doing so until he has walked away the distance he wishes to call the falcon. This shortfall can sometimes be overcome by putting the falcon down on a convenient perch, such as a gate or fence post or rail and then giving her a chick head to eat. Whilst she consumes this the falconer must sprint away as best he can with the lure ready to be swung immediately should the falcon start to come before he is ready. I do a great deal of my training on my own and therefore come across this problem all the time. Some falcons will eat the chick head and look around for more giving you ample time to get away. Others soon learn what you are doing and come with the chick head in their foot. My last Jerkin learnt this only too well. The other item that may help in such a situation is a portable T-perch. If you are on your own the fence post or gate you intend to put the falcon on might not be right as far as the wind direction is concerned. By taking a portable perch with you this is a problem that is easily overcome.

Once a falcon is coming instantly to the lure a decent distance, does not try and carry it and is good mannered when it comes to picking her back up off it, then the manner in which progression with the lure is to be taken would, at this point, traditionally vary depending on whether the falcon was to be flown out of the hood or used for waiting on flights. Those that tend to fly game, particularly in Europe, consider it akin to sacrilege to stoop a falcon to the lure that is intended for waiting on flights. They argue vociferously that to do so will discourage the falcon from mounting and indeed probably stop her even wanting to wait on at all but instead she will have a tendency to cruise around waiting for the lure to be produced.

Now it should be remembered the subject of this book is passage falcons, not eyasses. Regardless of future intended quarry I stoop freshly trained passage falcons to the lure without giving consideration as to whether they are destined for waiting on flights or out of the hood flights. The reason for this is a very simple one. Consider the time of year a passage falcon comes into the hands of the falconer. Granted, her training will take quite a bit longer than an eyass but she will be ready to be entered when the Game Season is some five or six months away at least. Having manned her down, got her flying to the lure, muscled her back up, do you really want her sitting round for almost half a year again before she is flown at quarry? Certainly this was not the policy of the Old Hawking Club and passage falcons, even those intended for grouse the following season, were flown out of the hood at rooks to keep them in work and strengthen the bond between falconer and falcon. If the passager could be successfully entered at rooks and flown hard for a couple of months, should he or she still have her, the falconer will have a prize indeed for later in the year. If this plan is followed then when her retraining commences in July she will be flown to the lure in a completely different manner and will very soon learn the different mode of flight required of her. I would just like to make one final point on the manner in which a falcon is exercised to the lure. I never ever ask any falcon of mine to do ground passes at the lure because I consider it to be wrong on two counts. Firstly, when the exercise session is finished I always make a loud shout of "Ho" and then throw the lure out on the ground. The falcon knows that no matter, what the lure is now hers and she can come in, alight on it without drama, and then take the small reward that almost invariably leads to a far bigger reward. Whereas, were I to ask her to do ground passes then throwing the lure out onto the ground at the end of the session, as I perceive it, would be devalued tremendously. The second reason I never do ground passes is the risk of injury to the falcon. Much easier for things to go wrong when the lure is on the ground and accordingly any misjudgement on the part of the falconer or falcon stands the chance of having quite severe consequences for the falcon. At this point it is probably worth repeating that I am not trying to claim in any part of my book that my way is the only way and that other ways and thoughts on training are wrong. I am merely pointing out what works for me and has done so over a great many years. Gilbert Blaine, undoubtedly one of the greatest falconers and game hawkers of recent times, invariably exercised his falcons by getting them to do ground passes at the lure. As much as I respect this falconer, probably above all others, in this particular instance I would have to disagree with him in the method he employed for exercising his falcons.

At this stage the passager will not be called off from the fist of an assistant but unhooded, allowed to take in her surroundings and then take off when she is good and ready to do so. Whereas the eyass will almost always have a rouse, mute, possibly rouse again and then go; the passager is more nervous in her manners for the first season or two at least and will normally have a quick glance round and launch herself from the fist. The one thing I never ever do is cast the falcon from the fist. This to me is a totally negative and complete unnecessary move on the part of the falconer and can only be something the falcon reflects on negatively. It has been taught for week after week that the fist is a safe and often rewarding environment and now here is the falconer physically hurling her off of it and just for what reason exactly. When it comes to flying quarry, will a couple of seconds make any difference what so ever if she is being flown at rooks. Will a few seconds really make all the difference between the falcon fetching the rooks and never getting on terms with them? If the answer is yes then the hawking is taking place in unsuitable circumstances and smacks of pot hunting as opposed to falconry. On the moors with a dog on point what possible difference can a few seconds make? In October when Grouse get jumpy then they are liable to burst at anytime and a few seconds makes no difference what so ever. For the falcon however these few seconds make a world of difference. She has the opportunity to weigh up the circumstances, ready herself physically as well as mentally for the flight and most important of all, leaves the falconers glove in a positive manner. The choice as to exactly when to leave the fist was hers and she takes off as and when she wants, as opposed to being hurled off in a brusque fashion as if being discarded. Just think how you would feel if you were driven to a venue to perform some task and the driver comes round and opens the passenger door to let you out and instead of waiting for you to disembark when ready they grabbed you and hauled you out. There is a chance you wouldn't think kindly of that driver. I realise I am probably labouring the point but I can never understand any falconer who spends a great deal of time building a decent working relationship with his falcon and then treats it in such a unkindly, and if we are honest unnecessary manner. To be fair the urge to launch the falcon as quickly as possible is probably fired by enthusiasm and not any sense of not caring, but the effect on the falcon is the same. It leaves the fist of the falconer in a negative manner.

A passage falcon that is intended for duck hawking, as with falconers in America, then flights at quarry will be taken on as soon as possible. Certainly here in Europe in general and the United Kingdom in particular, Duck hawking tends to be an incidental as opposed to the general quarry. Accordingly out of the hood flights at Rook will be the order of the day for at least a couple of months. Then the passager will be put down to moult and will be taken up again in sufficient time to get her on the wing again in time for the start of the game hawking season. Two things will be blatantly obvious to the falconer. The first is that passage falcons tend to moult very erratically and certainly the vast majority do not moult cleanly at their first attempt; which in turns means the falcon will have to be taken up from the moult looking somewhat of a mess aesthetically, but this really can't be helped as there is no sensible alternative. The second factor is that a slight degree of a differing approach will have to be used in the re-training of the falcon. It will now be required that she waits on instead of having the hood removed and launching herself at a quarry she can clearly see.

Initial retraining to the lure will be straight forward up to the point where the falcon is coming promptly to the swung lure at a decent distance. Now we progress to the stage were our passager is allowed to leave the fist freely of her own accord and hopefully she will circle us and not disappear into the blue yonder. Once this stage is reached it is time to progress with her guidance. As with an eyass she will be flown, if possible on a decent slope with an up draught on it and encouraged to circle by the falconer walking down the hill and into the wind. A keen eye must be kept on the falcon to ensure she is looking inwards towards the falconer and not trying to seek out something to fly at. This is not normally a problem with an eyass but of course a passager has flown quarry for several months unaided and is used to taking advantage of what she sees as an opportunity. Initially the falconer is looking to get just one or two circuits from the falcon and if all goes well this can be built gradually, till come the start of the game season she is staying on the wing long enough for a flush to be engineered beneath her. When I follow this regime I have a dog with me and make the dog sit when the falcon is flying, when I am ready to call the falcon in I call the dog and yell and wave my arms as if it was a genuine flush. Soon the falcon will undoubtedly take note of the stationary dog, even if it's true significance is not fully understood yet.

As mentioned earlier, for a falcon that is intended to be used as a game hawk, then stooping to the lure has always been considered an absolute cardinal sin. It should never ever be contemplated no matter what the circumstances. I myself slavishly followed this rule for many years without question. Like other falconers I would get a falcon flying loose and then ensure that I flew it on a slope that had a prevailing up draught. By casting the falcon off at the top of the slope and then walking down directly into the wind the falcon would supposedly circle above me and the wind direction would help lift the falcon. But what do you do when you have a young falcon ready to go free and there isn't a convenient hill with a prevailing wind blowing up it. Nowadays with the almost common place use of the kite or balloon this question seems superfluous, but it was not, of course, always so. It should also be taken into account that some falconers quite simply don't want to employ such artificial methods when training a falcon. Do you not fly her everyday that you can't fulfil these supposedly essential requirements or do you seek an acceptable alternative? I faced just such a dilemma several years ago with an eyass Gyr/ Peregrine hybrid male. So, I will admit initially very reluctantly, I stooped him to a lure for eleven consecutive days. After that I did I did have access to an ideal set up and proceeded with his training in the conventional way. I had grave doubts as to whether or not this falcon would ever be any good for game and was almost convinced I may have ruined him. It was not the case, nor has it been with the falcons I have trained for game since. I now stoop all new falcons to the lure until they are fit and muscled up. Then they go their separate ways with regard to training for out of the hood or waiting on flights. At the end of the moult I stoop my old game hawks to the lure for a period of around ten days to get them fit and back into fine fettle again.

With a young falcon that has been made fit by means of stooping to the lure the up draught from the side of a hill is just as appealing as it is to a falcon that has not been stooped to a lure. Especially so if the falcon is being flown over a point that eventually produces game. Falcons are intelligent creatures and very soon learn what gives them a good chance of a meal and what doesn't. In the case of seasoned game hawks they know full well the difference between being taken into a field with no dogs running and a lure being produced than being cast off on a moor with a pointer or setter beneath them.

There seems to have been a great deal of rubbish spoken and written over the years about making falcons lure bound. I have known of hardly any falcons that were truly lure bound. But I have known of several falconers that believed in such a thing and convinced themselves that a particular falcon was suffering from it. If a falcon is exercised to a lure for years on end without ever having been entered to quarry then it is hardly surprising that she doesn't instantly look for quarry when the hood is removed. She will need to be re-educated and taught that she can catch quarry. Her confidence, self belief and of course muscle tone, will have to be built up and she will have to have exceedingly advantageous slips sought for her. But with care and patience it can be done. I have had a Prairie Falcon given to me that had been used as a display falcon for five years. Twice a day, six days a week throughout the summer season she had been flown to a lure. Then at the end of the season she would be left idle on a block until the start of the following year.

When she was given to me she had several vices as well as being supposedly lure bound. She was simply awful to hood and dreadful to pick up off of a lure. The hooding was due to a variety of people with varying degrees of skill, or lack of it apparently, handling her during the display season. With a great deal of care and patience she eventually hooded as well as any falcon I have ever had. The mantling over the lure and trying to scurry away with it was obviously caused by being picked up very quickly and probably roughly from the lure and not being given sufficient time to take a suitable reward. This vice was overcome by treating her as if she had never seen a lure before and going through the whole introduction process only in an extremely exaggerated fashion. The meals on the lure were smaller than I would normally give and I would kneel down a little way off from her as she fed. I would ignore her completely as she fed and make no move what so ever to get closer or give her bechins. When she had finished the food on the lure she would then be encouraged to jump back up onto the glove and given a large meal there.

She was then stooped to a lure in the conventional manner but at the end of the session the lure was hidden a dead rook was thrown out. At first she seemed almost nervous of the corvid but eventually grabbed it when it was produced. Eventually she was entered to rooks and once she had killed two or three never looked back. I am not saying entering was straight forward and a great many slips were refused or flown half heartedly before success was finally achieved. But the perseverance paid off and this supposed lure bound nightmare of a falcon turned into an excellent hunting hawk.

Another falcon I knew of was given to a fellow falconer because it was lure bound and at the age of seventeen not worth bothering with anymore. It too had only ever been used in displays and now was being disposed of because it was old an unexciting. It would only ever fly to and fro to the lure, never made any height and never attacked the lure with any gusto. But then that was hardly surprising from the point of view of the falcon. The Sakret in question knew exactly what was going to happen day in and day out. It surprises me the boredom didn’t kill it. But once in the hands of a competent falconer the Sakret underwent a complete retraining process.

It was put down to moult and allowed to spend several months feeding on high quality food. At the end of the moult it was enseamed properly and then trained to a lure suspended from a kite. After much perseverance by both the falconer and the Sakret the lure would eventually be taken regularly at a height of around eight hundred feet. Once this was achieved the Sakret was given a chance and taken north to have some flights on a Grouse Moor. It unfortunately never managed to bring one to bag although it did knock two down and forced several to bail out. But on returning south it made a very good Partridge hawk and continued to do so for a further three seasons before unfortunately killing itself in a collision with a fence.

The reader will note that no mention has been made of the pole lure, a lure towed behind a model aircraft or even a radio controlled model of a quarry species. This is because I have tried the pole lure with various falcons, eyass and a single passage and whilst some of the smaller falcons seem to take well to a pole lure and fly it with vigour I have never been impressed with its usage when it comes to large falcons and the one passage falcon I tried to fly at it took a very distinct dislike to it. Again I harp back to the fact that I am probably very set in my ways and don't see any advantage in using a pole lure. With regard to lures towed behind model aircraft and artificial quarry models, I prefer to get a passage falcon back in the air as quickly as is consistent with solid training and believe the muscle it built up in the first few months of its life was at the level the falcon itself required for successful survival. Otherwise I believe the falcon would not be the topic of any discussion as it would have passed away.

Last but not least I have made no mention of the lure suspended from a kite or balloon as a method of training. Again, what people want to do when it comes to training and muscling up an eyass falcon is open to individual choice. There are those that swear by the use of the kite and there can be no argument that it is a very effective method of getting a falcon fit quite quickly. I personally have dabbled once or twice and had mixed results. Purely out of interest I will mention I flew a male Harris Hawk to the kite, not to any great height, less than seventy metres in fact, but the increase in fitness, most noticeable on initial acceleration, certainly made the effort worthwhile and would be something I would consider doing with this particular species again. However when it comes to passage falcons I think the quicker they are back on the wing flying real quarry the better. Nothing makes a falcon fitter than actual hunting.

FITNESS TRAINING AND ENTERING

Getting a passage falcon fit enough to fly quarry, unless there has been some very major drama in her training, should not take very long at all. She would have been at the absolute peak of fitness when she came into the hands of the falconer and her training, although considerably longer in duration than that of an eyas falcon, should not be so long as to have robbed the falcon of all her fitness and muscle tone. Yes she will have become a little flabby and her breath may be short when flown again for the first few times but both muscle tone and full use of air sacs will soon be back to their former and quite formidable powers.

For me it is a case of a no nonsense, straight forward regime of stooping the falcon to a conventional lure that I favour. When it comes to the lure itself I mean a thoroughly old fashioned lure in the shape of a somewhat stunted horseshoe that is on a line which in turn is itself connected to a lure stick. I do not out of choice use pole lure, kite, balloon or drone. I have indeed tried and played with them all at various times, however this is more out of curiosity rather than with any serious intent. Also it would be fair to say, that on reflection, those cases where I did have a little dabble would have been with domestically produced eyas falcons as opposed to passage falcons anyway. I did once play with a male Harris Hawk going up to a kite but the results of this were somewhat disappointing in that he seemed to set his own ceiling of around forty metres.

For me completely traditional lure work is the best way to get a passager back into hunting condition. When a falcon can make twenty or so really good hard and meaningful passes at the lure without opening its beak then I consider it ready to move on and attempt entering her. I am not really in favour of jumping the falcon to the fist from the floor repeatedly, as is often extensively used when training an eyas falcon or hawk. Whilst this undoubtedly does build muscle and stamina in a young hawk I wouldn't want to repeatedly ask a passage falcon to come to me for such a small reward. After all I am constantly mindful that this started life as a truly wild falcon and want all my interactions with her to appear positive ones in her favour. Some would argue that jump ups from the floor could still serve a useful purpose, such as when the weather was far from clement. I would counter argue, that with a passage falcon and getting out in order to give her exercise, there are not too many occasions when the weather in the form of rain or winds actually does manage to stop play. To do so the rain would have to be pretty heavy and constant. As with any hawk or falcon snow and fog are the two principal times when flying is temporarily put on hold. Once fit again, a passager revels in high winds and has the knowledge, from past experiences, to be able to deal with them and to some extent use them to her advantage.

I stoop passage falcons to the lure, no matter what their intended eventual quarry may be. That is either out of the hood at Rooks or waiting on for game such as Pheasant or Grouse. I can virtually hear the moans and groans as the previous two sentences are read by those who fly or intend to fly game with their falcon. They will no doubt be running through their minds that to stoop an intended game hawk to the lure is not the correct way to go about things and this course of action will have the very serious effect of eventually lowering the pitch of the falcon. With a great deal of respect I would say that in my opinion this train of thought, although a commonly held one, has very little hard evidence to back it up and certainly in my experience simply isn't the case.

It would appear that in the USA and certainly northern Mexico the primary quarry for passage falcons are ducks that are flown in a waiting on style. For these falcons then I can understand the logic behind the thinking that the falcon should not be stooped to the lure and the lure itself only used as a method of recall. Personally, I believe this is not a valid argument but then in these countries it should be borne in mind that the use of pigeons is considered the norm when training such falcons. I have stooped all my falcons to the lure in an effort to get them truly fit before trying to enter them and that includes falcons that are going to be entered at game. With an eyass then, the switch from being stooped to the lure on low ground, to being allowed to circle freely on high ground, with sensible use of natural up draughts, will certainly aid her education when it comes to waiting on for an unseen quarry. In the case of European falconers however, the passage falcon will come into the hands of the falconer when, by the time her training is complete and she is back on the wing, game will well and truly be out of season. This means she either sits idle for several months or instead is flown for a relatively short season at a quarry that is legal and offers a challenging as well as sporting flight. In most of Europe and certainly in the United Kingdom then, the quarry that presents itself as an abundant, easy to find and also to get permission to fly at, is the ubiquitous Rook.

The rook is actually a very under estimated quarry and one which deserves a great deal of respect when being considered for sporting purposes. Here I am meaning proper rook hawking where the flight is a true test of the fitness and determination of the falcon and not merely something at which an overmatched eyas hybrid falcon is unceremoniously thrown out of a vehicle window closely as possible to an intended victim. As this is not only illegal it is totally unsporting. The latter is not sport but merely an exercise in attempting to kill simply for the sake of it. To label this sporting travesty as rook hawking undermines the true sport shown by those that carry it out properly and also mars the memory of the likes of the Old Hawking Club who really did take this branch of the sport to an absolute Zenith, the like of which will be unlikely to be ever seen again.

If the passager is being trained and flown where ducks are going to be the principal quarry and pigeons have been used in its training then obviously getting a falcon over a duck pond at a reasonable height is not a particularly taxing matter and provided the falcon can be served regularly in the early days of hunting then she should improve almost flight by flight until she is steady in her mounting and approach and then can be relied upon to start showing some decent sport. When hawking with my friends in Mexico the thermals that are almost ever present are almost a god given gift to help even the laziest of falcons attain considerable height without expending too much energy. For a falcon that does want to hunt, then the thermals merely assist her in getting a really decent height very quickly indeed. Either way this sort of almost idyllic flying conditions have a tendency to bring about success and with success most certainly comes a degree of confidence. What I will say is that falconers must make the most of the conditions that they predominately have to work with. Some of the falcons that fly day in day out in conditions that allow thermalling do not necessarily fly well when asked to do so, when gaining height has to be achieved without the aid of nature's elevator.

I well remember being a judge at a Sky trial in Mexico many years ago when the sun remained hidden behind heavy cloud for two days and the wind was a great deal stronger than would normally have been expected in that region at that time of year. Many of the falcons entered in the trials failed to gain any decent height or even gain height at all within the parameters of the trial area. Those that did do well were hunting falcons that were simply at the top of their game and worked to gain height whether or not there were thermals to assist them. The fitness and confidence levels of these falcons were such that they wanted an opportunity to make a kill and worked hard to give themselves the best possible chance of doing so.

For those of us in the UK and most of Europe, game birds, most likely Grouse, will be the eventual intended aim for our passage falcon; so she will need to get fit and into hunting condition physically by means of the lure. Her mental outlook can be helped by the very simple expedient of a small addition when stopping the falcon to the lure. Quite simply it pays dividends to have several dead rooks in the freezer to which you have recourse as and when desired. There will be those that take great trouble garnishing their lures with the wings of rooks in the hopes that this will make the whole thing more attractive to the falcon and also focus her mind on black feathered birds. The idea is that when ready to be entered, the removal of the hood from the falcon and with black winged birds, the first thing the falcon sees this will somehow magically convince her to fly them with gusto. I do not garnish my lures with wings of any description, but will ensure that the basic body is dark when it comes to using it for an intended rook hawk. What I will do however, is have a dead rook with me that I throw out onto the ground at the end of the luring session. The rook would have been prepared so that the breast feathers are stripped back and some highly palatable meat, such as quail or pigeon breast, is secured in position. The falcon will take some mouthfuls of food from the last minute lure substitute and will not be put off by the taste of the rook. I have never had too much trouble with falcons disliking the taste of rook flesh but all the old works on falconry categorically state that falcons do not like it. I only carry out this deceptive ploy literally two or three times at most. It really is only a feel safe ploy more for my benefit than that of the falcon. However it is one of those habits that I do seem reluctant to let go of and probably really is a complete waste of time and effort on my part.

Falcon on lure

As already stated previously I don't throw the lure up in the air for the falcon to catch at the end of an exercising session as I feel it is an open invitation for an accident to occur to the falcon. Additionally, no bird ever throws itself up into the air when it thinks a falcon is about to take it and so the action can never be considered a natural one. Those that throw the lure up in the air at the end of a stooping to the lure session do so for their own satisfaction or to pander to their ego, particularly if others are watching. Should it be the case that knowledgeable falconers were watching they would probably not be thinking exceedingly complimentary thoughts on seeing such an action carried out. My practice is to throw the lure on the ground at the end of the work session and the falcon knows the lure is now hers, because this is the only time I ever throw the lure on the ground and I do so to an accompanying shout. When getting close to wanting to enter the passager to quarry then for the last few days of lure work sessions I throw out a dead rook instead of the lure itself, again accompanied by a very robust shout to signal to her that her work is done and now she is going to get her reward. Why throw out a dead rook instead of the lure itself? The reason is quite simply that a passage falcon that has obviously killed a great many times for herself seems to suddenly not understand what hunting is all about when the falconer tries to re-introduce her to it. If not prepared thoroughly they will often refuse slip after slip until the falconer finds himself wanting to pull his or her hair out in sheer frustration. The presentation of a carcase for her to initially feed on at the end of the luring session is like a half way house to the real thing. Old school falconers in years gone by would have given the passager a pigeon to kill at the block to supposedly switch her back on. Modern falconers, certainly within the UK anyway, don't do that sort of thing now or even condone it. It really isn't necessary when two or three occasions for the passage falcon to feed on a dead rook will have more or less the same effect. Also of course, with the falcon coming down in her agitated state, just having flown hard for her food, the carcase is a good test for the training you have done with her in relation to picking her up off of any future kills. It is much better to find out now if you need to retrace your steps a little and reinforce a particular lesson than when the blood is really up and the kill is for real.

For those that still have doubts in their minds as to whether or not the flying of a passage falcon at rooks for one season, albeit a relatively short one, is the right and proper way to go about things then I can only put forward an argument that convinced me many years ago that there was absolutely no harm in it. The Old Hawking Club, famed not only for the quantity of the sport they showed each season but also the very high quality of their endeavours, certainly drafted in a considerable number of fresh passage falcons each year. All of the fresh passagers would be entered at rooks and then later in the year sent north to be flown at grouse. Certainly it wasn't their findings that a falcon could only be flown at one or the other of these two totally different quarries requiring different styles of flying to bring them to the bag. Having got the passage falcon on the wing again and capable of flying hard and stooping well without her beak gaping in exertion it is time to try and get her entered as quickly as possible and get her back into the life of a hunting falcon again.

When it comes to entering the passager it is absolutely essential that the falconer pays just as much attention to the potential of any slips selected as he would with an eyas falcon. I know of several falconers in the past that have taken the attitude that being a passager the falcon already knows how to kill and given a fair opportunity will unhesitatingly do so again. This really is very far from the case in actual fact. It is as if the rest away from having to provide her own living has somehow quite literally switched her off and unless great care is taken in terms of her readiness, that is her physical and mental abilities, also the slips selected for her, then the almost inevitable result will be abject failure. When selecting slips for the first few occasions sporting flights should be the furthest thing from the mind of the falconer. What is being sought are easy opportunities for the falcon to make a kill and taste warm flesh and blood again as well as feel the tremble of another life within the grasp of her feet. Nothing seems to excite a falcon more than this, particularly the last element in the equation. Slips that would be ideal, and because they are ideal then

Murphy's law will make them almost impossible to find, are rooks that are out in the fields feeding but soaking wet from a truly heavy shower. Rooks that are obviously injured or impaired in some way or are really long way out in the open and consequently a very great distance away from cover. Anything in fact that acts as an impediment to the rook and gives the falcon a more than even chance of being successful. Any advantage that can be made the most of is what would be sought. Once two or three kills are under the belt then slips can start being selective with the emphasis on sport as opposed to end result. Early kills are vital though to get the falcon confident in her own abilities again and back into the mind set of believing in her own prowess when it comes to hunting.

As well as trying to find slips that are heavily loaded in favour of the falcon in the early stages the basic rules of slipping a rook hawk should also not be forgotten. These are well known and need only scant mention here more as a general reminder than a manual laid out for reference. Always make sure the slip is directly into the wind so as to allow the falcon to put her powers of flight to good use and put into play the slight natural advantage bestowed on her by evolution of the centuries. Directly into the wind does mean precisely that, slips that have been attempted through a cross wind rarely end in success and if by some amazing piece of luck they do then they have taught the falcon a negative lesson in that she can catch rooks by turning across the wind on occasions.

Always ensure the rooks are at the very minimum twice as far from cover as they are from the falcon at the moment of slipping. In actual fact, particularly in the early days of a new hunting relationship, then three times the distance would be a far better yardstick. If there is any cover within reach, be it trees, buildings, bushes or even thick hedges then slipping should not be considered. Slips of the ideal length mentioned will never be easy to find but holding out for such slips would pay dividends in the long run. As difficult as it is to turn down what appear initially to be perfectly good slips, it is better to err on the side of caution than discourage the falcon by giving her opportunities that realistically have very little chance of success. I can remember when I first started to fly falcons accompanying someone with a passage falcon looking for a decent slip. We spent all day spotting rooks and on each occasion the possible slip would be rejected by my companion for whatever reason he thought applicable. I am ashamed to say in my own mind I was convinced he was simply looking for an excuse not to fly at all. In actual fact I demonstrated my own ignorance in not realising that this man was striving for the very best opportunity for his falcon and was showing me more knowledge by the slips he refused, than by those he could have taken on. The following day he found a slip that he thought suited his purpose and a fine kill followed, rather proving his point and compounding my own short comings. Let me also state here that exceptionally close slips can often not be the golden opportunities they appear. A falcon that is not experienced with rooks will very soon find just how quickly a rook can slip round her and all of a sudden we have a downwind flight without the falcon having gained any form of advantage before it became so from an upwind slip.

Slipping at mixed flocks of rooks, jackdaws, starlings and perhaps crows is definitely to be avoided. The confusing melee that would inevitably follow the slip could well turn into either a falcon that has to be tracked down or one that

Megan, intermewed falcon

finds itself with a fight on its hands if there are several crows within the mixed flock. Also never slip if there are more rooks visible either on your flanks or downwind of you. If you have selected the rooks that are dead ahead and, in your mind anyway, perfectly placed, doesn't mean the falcon will look at the scenario in quite the same way. Also, do not slip until the rooks have actually taken to the air. It tends to be movement that stimulates a predator and rooks feeding on the ground rarely move sufficiently to excite the falcon to the point of taking them on in earnest. Just walking towards the rooks as they feed, with the braces of the hood struck, should be sufficient to ensure a flight will eventually ensue. It also hardly requires mentioning but I will do so for the sake of clarity, do not slip at a rook that is on passage, which is a single rook flying from distant point to distant point with an obvious purpose. These are a challenging flight for even the most experienced rook hawks and hardly one to even contemplate with a falcon you are trying to enter.

Once the passage falcon has been entered and several kills have been credited to her then the falconer can start to look for better and more sporting flights. The really advantageous slips were merely a means to an end and can't really be considered as sport. It is after this necessary education period has been completed that the real sport can begin. My own circumstances, back in the days when passage falcons from abroad were relatively freely available and certainly legal, meant that I was almost spoilt in the number of suitable slips that I could engineer on an almost daily basis. It would be true to say I had almost the perfect scenario at my disposal when it came to entering a new falcon to rooks. In those days I flew mainly passage Saker Falcons from Pakistan at rooks and these would come over to England, normally requiring to be imped and generally cleaned up before contemplating trying to fly them. Once trained and ready to be entered I would go to my local pig farm that still farmed in the old fashioned way with pigs outside in small groups in fenced off divisions of approximately thirty foot square, separated by low voltage electric fences. The pigs would be feed processed food once a day at a regular time and accordingly great numbers of rooks would gather to take advantage of spillage and natural wastage.

Within this black melee that descended on the farm would always be a few rooks that couldn't fly as well as their companions and when the flock took fright and made off, any falcon worth its salt would instantly pick out the weakling or the sickly rook and have something of a relatively easy kill. These early flights could hardly be classed as sport I am the first to admit, but two or three of these kills would give the falcon a good education and the confidence to take on rooks in more conventional environment.

Just as a little parting thought for this chapter I would add that if ever you would like to experience firsthand the rage and indignation a falcon is capable of expressing then train a passage Saker Falcon or indeed, if you have a masochistic streak, then a passage Prairie Falcon. Both will teach you about your own limits when it comes to patience and tolerance and also which antiseptic creams work best when dealing with repeated bites from falcons.

OUT OF THE HOOD FLIGHTS

Historically the classic flight for the passage falcon that offered the most comprehensive test of bravery, stamina, determination and fitness, has been with the Red kite as the intended quarry. At least this was always the case with British falconers, on the European mainland and indeed India as it was then; or rather to some degree still is, the black Kite that attracts the attention of the falconer seeking the ultimate test for his falcons. This flight entailed the use of a cast of falcons and required that it be followed on horseback due the distances that could very rapidly be covered by both pursued as well as pursuers. Flights often lasted several miles and could easily and all too often result in the loss of a falcon or indeed both members of the cast. Falconers of old, unlike their modern counterparts, did not have the back up and undeniable feeling of reassurance of a competent telemetry set when out hawking. For our forefathers looking for a lost hawk was a very different affair from the somewhat high Tec exercise it has now become. Although obviously searching for a lost falcon is still a somewhat fraught affair, at least with the aid of telemetry, it can continue after dark and also great distances can be checked out very quickly by getting to some high point and sweeping the surrounding countryside.

For the falconers of old it was a very different scenario and required a great deal of luck, as well as skill to recover the wayward falcon. They needed to keep the flight within sight, if at all possible, and should the flight go far and fast then the old natural methods of locating the falcons, either with or without their intended prey, would be brought into play. Some were very straight forward such as rooks ringing up skywards very noisily, wood pigeons suddenly veering in their flight path, seagulls stooping repeatedly over the same spot, magpies chattering incessantly and hopping from tree to tree. Others were somewhat subtler with blackbirds sneaking along hedgerows and then bursting from the safety of the cover that had been shielding them from sight and going off with a loud frenetic calling. Cows suddenly congregating in the middle of a field would be another indicator, in fact anything that seemed out of place or slightly amiss in the natural order of things. The flight would have almost certainly gone downwind and at least the direction in which to look was normally a relatively straight forward one. In fact it was common practice to station riders, equipped with lures and spare hoods, at intervals downwind in the hopes of avoiding the loss of any falcons.

In the 17th and 18th centuries the Red kite was a very common bird in the UK and also in parts of Europe. Where it wasn't to be found in Europe then it would normally be replaced by the smaller but equally as aerial Black kite. Obviously there was no equivalent flight in what was to become the USA, as at the time the country itself was still being settled and those engaged in doing so had neither the knowledge or the inclination to practice a field sport purely for its own sake. Life was too harsh and immediate for such indulgences. Falconry wouldn't find a home in that particular region for another couple of hundred years or so. The population numbers and physical presence over such a large part of the UK meant that the Red kite was a quarry that could more or less always be found in country that was suitable for the flight and allowing the enthusiastic field to follow quite freely. East Anglia was an area that was to prove to be particularly popular with those that tended to specialise in this branch of the sport, as were the Berkshire Downs and parts of Yorkshire and Northumberland, particularly the edges of the moorlands.

It would appear from older works on falconry that the normal method of flying this particular quarry would be as follows. A tame eagle owl would be tethered out in the open and kites that were in the vicinity would very soon come to mob it. If for whatever reason the kites did not come in sufficiently close to mob the owl then the normal practice was to attach the brush of a fox to the jesses of the owl and let it fly a short distance on a creance, as if it were trying to make off with some large prey item secured in its grasp. This most certainly would not be ignored by any kites within the vicinity and soon they would be wheeling around above the presumably, somewhat bewildered, owl. Once a kite was within a reasonable distance a falcon would be slipped and it would make after the kite. Once the falcon and kite had separated themselves from any other kites that were immediately to hand the second falcon would be unhooded and then slipped. From that point on the flight would be joined in earnest, whereas up until then, the kite itself would probably not have felt in any particular danger and may even have put in one or two retaliatory stoops at the falcon. Almost certainly in a one against one situation the agility of the kite and its ability to mount so rapidly with such little effort would have more or less guaranteed its safe escape. With two falcons wanting to come to terms with it however, the kite would instinctively try and make good its escape and this it would do by ringing up to a tremendous height, often out of sight to the naked eye. Whilst rising, it would also be drifting downwind at a considerable rate and the field would have to have their wits about them to keep the flight within sight.

Eventually the falcons would fetch their quarry and then put such pressure on the kite as to make it seek refuge in a tree or in some shrubbery. From this point on the falcons would have gained the upper hand and would be putting in alternative stoops at the kite. Whether or not the kite was taken depended on the footing ability of the falcons and the evasion skills of the kite. As with so many flights in falconry the kill ratio was supposedly relatively poor, if catching quarry was the only important thing, however the sport itself was simply superb and showed off the very best of the flying capabilities of both the falcons themselves as well as the kites. The flying capabilities of the Red kite were held in such very high esteem by falconers in the 16th and 17th centuries that apparently it was not an unusual practice for three falcons to be slipped at an individual kite not just a cast. This must have been a very difficult flight to manage for the field should one of the falcons decide to fly at check or even indeed engage with another kite.

Passage Gyr falcons were often used for this flight as well as passage peregrines. Many believe, certainly within the older works on falconry, that the passing of this particular flight took with it the secret of getting the very best out of passage Gyr falcons and the true art of training them and bringing them into good flying condition. Certainly until the late 20th and early 21st century Gyrs were considered, in the main and by the majority of falconers, something more to be dabbled with than taken seriously for true falconry purposes. Probably one of the last truly dedicated followers of kite hawking in Britain was Colonel Thornton, who succeeded Lord Orford as manager of The Falconers' Club and renamed it The Confederate Hawks of Britain. He flew passage Gyrs as well as passage falcons at Red kites and it was generally assumed that when Edward Newcombe discovered old hawk trapper's huts at Dovrefjeld in Norway, these had been used decades previously to provide Lord Orford and Colonel Thornton with their passage Gyr falcons. All too soon though, circumstances changed in Britain. Kites became a great deal scarcer, large tracts of open land were broken up and divided into small farms under the enclosures act and generally the flight became more or less impossible to practice with any degree of quality or chance of success. Accordingly kite hawking quite rapidly passed from being a living breathing sport to become merely a few lines in the history books.

Up until recently the flight at Black kite was still practised by Indian falconers but the falcon they used in the main was the passage Saker falcon as opposed to the passage peregrine. I have had one or two letters from falconers in India informing me that falconry is still practised there on a very limited scale and at least one falconer has communicated to me he is flying Black kites with passage falcons. However, as falconry itself is illegal in India and has been for some time, I find this a somewhat dubious claim, added to the fact that no photos or detailed descriptions of any flights ever accompany these letters. When watching documentaries on India, particularly on the plains regions, it is evident that the countryside still lends itself very much to the practice of the flight, coupled to the fact that there really is no shortage of kites to fly at.

With the kite more or less removed as a quarry species in Britain a replacement quarry had to be found for Le Haut Vol (the high flight) that would test the prowess of a cast of trained falcons to a suitable degree and offer a truly fair and sporting flight. The answer came in the form of The Grey heron, a bird common in Britain and across mainland Europe. The countryside in which to fly such a quarry still needed to be as open as possible, but not to the great extent that had been required for the flight at kites. Herons themselves were easier to find and by managing heronries effectively, the falconer could ensure himself of a continuing source of flights for the future. This is exactly what falconers of the calibre of Edward Newcombe did as well as looking to mainland Europe to expand their field of sport. In 1839 Newcombe helped establish The Royal Loo Hawking Club whose sole purpose was to fly herons with style and in a true sporting manner. The kill was almost unimportant and in fact everything possible was done to spare the life of any heron taken by the falcons and wherever possible release it again.

Heron hawking became the pinnacle of the longwingers sport and it was the passage falcon that quite rightly took pride of place in the Hawkhouse, the mews and on the weathering ground. A few passage Gyr falcons were in fact tried at this flight but if the Gyrs could be induced to fly the herons with any degree of gusto then they almost invariably harmed them so much that they could not subsequently be released. Other than for one or two very noticeable exceptions the passage falcon was the only falcon used by the club and indeed by Newcombe himself when flying herons back in Britain.

The flight itself followed very much the lines of that employed against the kite, except a heron would first be slipped at whilst it was on passage, ie flying between its heronry and feeding ground. A single falcon would be slipped initially and once it had engaged the heron a second falcon would also then be slipped. There would then ensue a ringing flight as each side of the battle tried to gain supremacy over the other by ringing ever higher. If the falcons did not work hard to gain height advantage over the heron, then they would see their quarry drift away downwind as it gained height and would eventually be lost to them. But, if they won the battle of ringing for position then they would be in a position to start stooping at the heron. With each stoop the heron would, by avoiding the attentions of the falcon, lower its own pitch and the falcon would go back to her original height from the impetus of the throw up. In effect each stoop became more dangerous than the previous one.

Eventually the heron would either make the safety of some water, or would be taken by the falcons. Normally the passage falcons could be induced to step up off of the heron without damaging it too severely, other than in the pride department. With a check over, the heron was normally judged to be in a fit enough state to be allowed to go on its way again. Let me state here that I have often read how falcons are at a very real and severe risk of being stabbed by the long pointed beak of a heron and I have even read that many falcons have indeed been effectively speared by a heron with the beak. Having been privileged enough to see quite a large number of herons taken by falcons this genuinely is something I have not only never seen, but have never seen attempted either. In my humble opinion, gained from firsthand experience in the field, the beak of the heron represents a danger in that the heron will try

Intermewed Falcon on Rook

and grab the wing of the falcon in its beak and then endeavour to shake the falcon off itself. I have seen this done and the falcon concerned was out of action for the rest of the relatively short season with what was effectively a sprained wing. The real danger to a falcon fighting with a heron comes not from the beak but from the legs and feet of the heron. The legs are long and, by the very nature of the bird and how it hunts; the spread of the foot is indeed quite large. The heron, even before being brought fully to the ground by the falcon or cast of falcons will try its very best to kick the falcons off by swinging wildly with its feet. The legs of a heron are powerful and should not be under estimated. This alone makes it imperative that the falconer strive to get to the falcons and their prey as quickly as possible.

As with Kite hawking areas suitable for flying herons and finding herons in sufficient numbers and a legal situation in which to fly them dwindled to make the flight an impractical one. Certainly maintaining two or three casts of falcons purely for this flight was beyond ridiculous and the sport slowly wound itself down. In certain parts of mainland Europe the flight at heron is still a perfectly legal, albeit under the limitations of a special licence, normally granted in relation to fish farming operations. However, the lacking ingredient is going to be the passage falcon. Again we have a flight that was considered an absolute classic, and having enjoyed it many times myself first hand I have to say I totally agree, that is slowly making its way into the history books. Effectively in Britain the flight became more or less a thing of the past in the mid 19th century and, just as with the demise of kite hawking, a suitable replacement was sought.

Although normally only requiring a single passage falcon, and not a cast, rook hawking became the latest medium by which passagers could show their prowess in the field. It was a flight that offered true sport in its proper sense in that both prey and predator were strong fliers and quite evenly matched. We are talking here proper rook hawking, that is slipping a falcon at a rook that is on passage between its rookeries and feeding ground or vice versa. The rook is already well up, flying strongly and in an area it knows very well indeed. The falcon is unhooded and allowed to take to the air and begin her attack as and when she feels ready. In a somewhat reduced form the flight at rook would closely resemble the flight at heron in that normally an attack by the falcon was not truly direct, but the falcon would fly in the general direction of its quarry whilst all the time be striving to gain a height advantage as well as eventually fetch the rook.

Once the falcon had indeed fetched her rook at a decent height, the flight proper would begin and the almost balletic battle would unfold. With a single falcon against a single rook if the flight did end in success for the falcon, then

I am afraid it most certainly resulted in the death of the rook. Rooks fight hard for their lives, and why shouldn't they, the falcon fights equally hard to subdue them and accordingly the rook generally succumbs on the ground to the physical powers of the falcon. A good flight was certainly capable of lasting a mile or more and would be a fine test for a fit and healthy falcon and would surely highlight any weaknesses she may have in terms of fitness, or heart for the flight. The months of March and April were the traditional ones for rook hawking and the combination of weather conditions, fitness of both prey and predator, normally ensured that first class sport was the end result. This was the time of year when rooks were at their physical peak and long journeys were being made between feeding grounds and rookeries.

Again with the constant changing farming conditions, the ever increasing population of the country and the need for more and more land to be turned over from agricultural use to housing and support infra structure, rook hawking itself has had to change and change very much indeed. Following on horseback, in all but a very few remote areas, has become simply impossible and the four wheel drive vehicle has had to replace it. Nothing wrong with that in itself and generally a vehicle is a lot less trouble out in the field than a horse, certainly in my case anyway, as I have a very strong tendency to fall off of them. However, with the four wheel drive vehicle has come a side of falconry that I quite simply detest. That is launching a falcon out of the window of a moving car while it is still being driven towards the rooks that are feeding on the ground. This method of slipping is certainly illegal in the UK but is without doubt practised on a regular basis in other countries. Normally the vehicle has been manoeuvred into a position where the slip itself is a relatively close one and this is because the countryside simply isn't open enough for a proper slip and flight to be engaged in. If cover for the rooks is not too far away a close slip has to be sought in order for the falcon to stand a chance of fetching the rooks and turning them downwind before they reach cover. This is far more smash and grab than rook hawking proper. For me, throwing falcons out of car windows is not sport and it certainly isn't falconry. Should this be a tactic that someone would consider a fair and legitimate one then I would think that in these conditions a male Goshawk or even a male Harris Hawk would be better suited to the task.

The loss of really ideal rook hawking country more or less coincided with the loss of passage falcons to falconers in Britain and so a long, and at times, very glorious chapter in falconry came to something of a less than satisfactory end. The possibilities in Britain are now an unrealistic prospect that doesn't mean the young dedicated falconer can't pursue his dream elsewhere. I certainly do, and I am past my prime (that's a polite way of saying getting too long in the tooth) so no reason for a youngster not to make a concerted effort, even if it requires uprooting for a season or two, to enjoy the best that falconry has to offer before the opportunities fade away altogether.

For those lucky enough to get the opportunity to fly a passage falcon because it has been passed onto to them in hopes of eventually rehabilitating it then life has most definitely smiled on you. I am going to make the assumption that once it has been brought to the falconer that, other than perhaps completing a course of medication, the falcon itself is ready to be trained and the process of getting it back into the wild will therefore start with immediate effect. In this case the moral high ground of falconry and the seeking of the most aesthetically pleasing and rewarding flights is thrown straight out of the window. The idea is to get the falcon flying and fit and back to killing for herself as soon as possible and when she has shown she is capable of fending for herself then she should be set free. Or, as is often misquoted from Othello act 3 scene 3, "Though that her jesses were my dear heartstrings, I'd whistle her off down the wind to prey at fortune". After all she belongs in the wild and although the temptation to hang just a little longer on to a passage or haggard falcon that is being rehabilitated is always a strong one, the falconer needs to anticipate and savour the joy he or she will receive when they see that falcon set out on life's course again, due partially to their efforts.

I cannot put into words the joy felt when removing all the furniture from a passage or haggard falcon that would have been doomed yet through the efforts of man is getting another chance. Whether it is a case of taking equipment off and letting the falcon take to the wing from the glove, or cutting her furniture off as she feeds up on a kill, the feeling of satisfaction is immense and certainly worth all the effort that went into getting her to that stage.

Xena the Lanner Falcon on a rook

WAITING ON FLIGHTS

The theory of a waiting on flight is an extremely simple one in that game is located with either a dog or binoculars, the falcon is allowed to take to the wing and whilst she makes her pitch the falconer heads the point, or positions himself correctly in the case of finding game with binoculars, and when everything is set fair the quarry is flushed. On paper the inevitable result of this straight forward and easy to execute exercise is a blinding stoop, contact with the quarry and another head of game brought to bag. The actuality of the situation tends to vary a great deal from the supposed straight forward scenario in that there a myriad of things that can, and often do, go wrong.

We will work on the assumption that the falconer does have a falcon that can under normal circumstances, make a decent pitch more or less over his head and having done so, is constantly watching his every move for tell tale movements of the flushing of potential quarry. Then, other than drifting off too far from the point or suddenly flying at check, her presence will normally be sufficient to help keep the quarry where it should be. However that does not mean that given the slightest opportunity the quarry won't take advantage of the falcon drifting just a shade too far and jump into the air at what, from the falconer's point of view, is totally the wrong moment, making off like bullets down wind. Or, if in deep cover such as old heather, they may well sneak away ahead of the dog and separate making re-pointing them extremely difficult for the dog. Whether the falconer uses a Spaniel for flushing or, as more and more modern falconers tend to do, they teach the Pointer to flush on command, in the heat of an anticipated flush many falconers suddenly think they have developed noses better than those of their dogs and run round like headless chickens trying to flush the quarry themselves. This is almost invariably a mistake and if you don't trust your dogs you shouldn't surely be hawking with them. As I say, there are many things that can go wrong and what looks like an ideal and very promising set up can all too easily degenerate into something of a farce.

Let's just quickly look in a little more detail at these possible causes of a potentially good flight ending in something of a non event. Firstly the falcon we are concerned with here is a passager and has spent her time in the wild hunting for herself by spotting a potential victim and then chasing and catching it. She will no doubt have been unsuccessful far more times that she has been successful and will accordingly have decided there are certain quarries she can catch and certain ones where she stands very little chance. She will have also learnt the importance of wind conditions, position of the sun in relation to her stoop and elements of the terrain that will have a direct effect on her flight. The one common denominator in all her flights, whether with a successful outcome or not, is that she attacked a quarry that she could see right from the beginning of the flight. She does not hunt in a speculative manner as would a kestrel. Accordingly for her, being asked to fly round in anticipation that eventually something will be presented for her to fly at is, to say the least, not easy. In countries where the use of pigeons is allowed, then I suppose the task is considerably easier. Particularly so, if the pigeons are used judicially on the terrain where future hunting will take place and with pointing dogs present, then teaching the anticipation of impending quarry and the need for height to control it is not overly difficult.

For those that cannot legally use pigeons as a training aid or prefer, from an ethical point of view, not to use them then there is no alternative other than to train the falcon on a moor or partridge manor and over a point. By using experience gained over the years the falconer can bring about a flush at the best possible moment of each of these early flights for the falcon, in a way that offers her perhaps the chance of a decent chase if not a kill itself. The most important thing is to teach the falcon that it is the combination of man and dog that do present quarry and that from her point of view height and position are the make or break when it comes to success, or at least a very major part of it.

Next up in our examination comes the dog or, as in most cases, dogs. A dog that has a tendency to false point or be a little exuberant in its desire to flush the game should be avoided at all costs. If ever a steady reliable dog was called for this is the time. A good dog can make a falcon and equally certain is that an unreliable dog can ruin one forever. However, for the falconer that uses his canine companions to flush quarry, either directly with the pointer or with the aid of a spaniel, never will the timing of the flush be more important than with these first few flights at game with the passage falcon. Timing is everything and all is potentially won or lost on the flush. Three or four days of things going well and the falcon will have a sound base on which to build her experience and understanding of game hawking. Equally true, is that the same amount of time with things going wrong and not according to plan will see the falcon confused and unsure of what to expect and therefore flying at check will now become even more attractive to her than ever. Especially as, in her mind, flying check is how she provided for herself previously and did well enough out of it to survive.

Tiercel and Pointer

Firmly in the forefront of things that can potentially ruin a decent flight is the falconer, who it would probably be fair to say, must take pride of place; potentially being the loose cannon that can so easily affect the outcome in either a positive or negative way with, I would say, the emphasis leaning more towards the latter. The human element always seems to be bold and confident pre flight and this confident, nerves of steel attitude seems to diminish when actually dealing with the real thing. Confidence in the ability of the dogs to find, hold and then flush game unaided by a human, with a pathetic sense of smell in comparison to them, seems to evaporate when the first few crucial flights are being undertaken. Same is true in the confidence the falconer has in the ability of the falcon to circle and position herself and he is then constantly checking her position and may well, under this pressure, resort to trying to call her over quicker that the natural flow of things would bring about anyway. If by waving a hand or even glove then perhaps this would be acceptable, but only just. Any other method is a definite no go and will only teach the falcon that the moment the hand of the falconer goes anywhere near his pocket or bag she should make her way in quickly for a possible easy meal.

The bottom line is the falconer should have confidence in his dog, allow his falcon to actually fly and not just hang around his head and lastly and, perhaps most importantly of all, have confidence in his own abilities. He has after all brought things about, by using his skill in understanding the needs of the falcon and guiding her to this point, where a decent flight is in the process of being engineered. He should have faith in himself and stick to his plan.

Let us suppose that after a number of flights luck has decided to give the falconer a helping hand and a kill has resulted. It may not go down in the annals of falconry as one of the great flights, or even a mediocre one, but for the falcon it is a major day in her education and should be treated as such. She needs to get a really decent reward and should be fed there and then on the kill, as much as is consistent with her flying again the next day. It is of the utmost importance that the falconer gets down and assists his falcon with the meal. Her equipment can be changed and she can be made secure as she eats and the falconer can make an exaggerated point of giving her bechins. Never forget that the hold a falconer has over a passage falcon is always going to be somewhat tenuous and that everything possible should be done to keep the level of tameness, which the falconer worked so hard to establish, at its height. All too soon, a passage or haggard falcon can revert to its wild instincts and appear frightened by the mere presence of the falconer or indeed the dogs. From the point of view of the falcon her easiest way of dealing with this is quite simply to fly off, preferably taking her hard won kill with her. This would be nothing short of a disaster and will undoubtedly lead to the loss of the falcon, if not on this occasion then certainly within a very short time frame. Once these negative seeds are sown it is almost impossible to undo the harm done.

Not just in these early days but for the life of the working relationship between passage falcon and falconer even bring down to the lure and the subsequent picking up from it should be treated as an exercise in taming. Make the return of the falcon something more than just a few mouthfuls of food from the lure. Make the whole process a pleasant thing in her eyes and an experience to be enjoyed. Her tastes in life and also her expectations are relatively simple and straightforward. She wants to feed with minimum fuss and wants to feel safe and secure. The falconer should delight in being able to bring about this state of mind within the falcon. Even though the passage falcon has been very carefully and thoroughly introduced to dogs do not let them rush up to her when she is on the ground and therefore feeling at her most vulnerable. Also be sure in your mind that falcons most certainly can and do identify individual dogs. It is no good thinking that because you may have two black and white pointers that the falcon will accept all pointers and black and whites ones in particular as a matter of course. They certainly will not. I had a haggard falcon for rehabilitation that would sit out on its high perch as my two English Setters and two Pointers ran round and ignored her. The falcon would for her part sit with one foot tucked up totally unconcerned as to what they were doing. However if a friend visited me, who had the sister to one of my Setters, my falcon was alert and on her guard the whole time even though the visiting setter ignored her completely. The falcon unquestionably recognised the fact that this was a different dog and did not feel the same towards it.

When a passage falcon has made a kill, due to dog work, I do let the dogs approach closely but endeavour to keep myself between the dogs and the falcon. After all it is important that the dogs also get their reward for working well and need to feel part of the team. I am a great believer in the fact that dogs like to work for you and if rewarded strive harder to please you. Some may laugh either inwardly or out loud at this idea, neither of which I can assure you will bother me for one iota of time, but it is what I firmly believe and shall continue to do so. Happy dogs work harder in my opinion and anyway why not have a happy team as opposed to merely an obedient one. I try and employ the same in the home life of the falcon and dogs when they are not working. Meal times tend to be communial and the falcon is fed on the fist with the dogs milling around and getting treats. Familiarity in this case can lead to harmony in the field and at home, which has to be the desirable state.

It should also be born in mind that entering a passager at grouse or other game species will in the UK be very different to abroad. Let me explain fully exactly what I mean. In the UK we are no longer allowed to take or import passage falcons and accordingly the falcon we are trying to enter will be a rehabilitation case. There are occasions when indeed a falcon can be flown to a certain degree at game but is essentially not in a completely fit state to be released again back into the wild. I myself had a passage tiercel and flew him at grouse for 11 years with quite a degree of success. Initially the tiercel had been taken in because he had suffered a broken wing; it was thought as a result of a collision with power lines. The wing had been strapped and not pinned and as a result never set completely true. The tiercel was passed to me and after a very heavy imping session was eventually trained and got onto the wing again. The tiercel would fly with gusto one day but the following day would sit with his wing drooping and be reluctant to fly. The third day back on the wing flying again and fourth day no flying and so on. We worked out a schedule to use this routine to his and my advantage. The tiercel would be flown at grouse on day one and given a full crop of good food. This would be regardless of whether he achieved a kill or not. The only difference was that if he killed he was fed up on the kill with plenty of bechins etc. If he hadn't killed he would be taken up from the lure, again with bechins and absolutely no rush, but would be fed the majority of his meal on the fist once we got home. The following day would be a light feed on the fist and then next day out hunting again. This worked well for him and meant he got to fly quarry three days a week. I lived in Scotland at the time and although it was legal to hunt grouse on a Sunday I felt that dogs, hawks, quarry and falconers all needed one day of rest and accordingly only hunted six days a week.

Probably the majority of passage falcons that now find their way into the hands of UK falconers can be released back into the wild once they are truly

Tiercels in the field

fit and killing again. Therefore, with them entering to a game bird such as grouse will not ever really come into the equation because the time of year they will come into the hands of the falconer will be outside the game season. However, there will be those that either through injury or sickness have been with the falconer for some time and therefore game may well be an option to enter the falcon to and thereby judge her fitness and probability of a successful release. In such cases entering to game will not be easy initially, for all the reasons stated earlier such as check, but once she has been entered, only a few successful kills will be required before the falcon can be released and allowed to go on her way. A falcon that was brought in later in the season and was considered unfit for release, but fit enough to show some sport, would be entered at rooks before being put down to moult. Once equipped with new feathers entering her at game would be paramount and the procedure would be as described earlier in the chapter. For those that claim this is rubbish and that a rook hawk will not make a game hawk then I can only assume you criticise from what you have read not from what you have experienced. The current mind set appears to be that you cannot switch a falcon from flying quarry out of the hood to waiting on. This just isn't so and certainly was the routine practice of The Old Hawking Club.

For me whatever species is legally available and in sufficiently abundant supply at the time the passager needs entering then that is what I will choose. For a falcon that can continue to be flown but not released then certainly you can switch quarries at a later date. It is important to get a passager back up and flying and more importantly killing again as quickly as possible. The one thing that always amazes me is that how after being in captivity even for a short period of time the passage falcon seems to have forgotten how to kill and in fact lost the desire completely to do so.

For those with passage falcons in the States or indeed Mexico then ducks are normally the quarry the falcon will be entered at. Whilst the flight is indeed a waiting on one the falcon can at least see the ducks within seconds of leaving the fist and would most probably have hunted them before coming into partnership with man. Also assisting the falcon to a very great degree, particularly in Mexico, will be the thermals that help a falcon to tremendous heights with very little effort on her part. I have seen flights in Mexico where the falcon has gone to such heights as to knock three ducks down out of the same flush. The first was killed dead in the stoop. The second was cut down after a huge throw up from the first stoop and the falcon then used her impetus to go straight for a third duck instead of throwing up. She was successful with this manoeuvre and bound to the third duck. I have also seen the same falcon go high and when two male Pintail ducks were flushed she killed the first dead in the stoop and took the second after stooping again from the throw up. This is a hard quarry for a falcon to take, let alone two from the same flush. Flying ducks in the UK tends, for most falconers it seems, to be an incidental as opposed to a primary quarry. We don't seem to have the small man made ponds that have been dug to enable cattle to drink. Ducks in the UK tend either to be found on large expanses of water or in rivers.

Flying grouse, partridge and pheasant are the normal game flights that the passage falcon would be used for in Britain. For me personally, and I don't wish deliberately to upset those that enjoy it, flying pheasants with falcons is not a great deal of fun. A pheasant is a big and colourful bird and if you can get them to flush in the open not particularly difficult for a falcon to take. The falcon needs to be strong and have courage, a cock pheasant is a very formidable adversary on the ground, but avoiding the stoop is not the pheasant's strong point. Providing the falcon hits the pheasant hard initially, most of the struggle on the ground is a relatively futile one. As I say, taste is a personal thing and to each their own and pheasant hawking for me has always been an incidental alongside grouse or partridge hawking.

Partridge hawking with a passage falcon is something of an over kill and the flight is better suited to a tiercel. Even so I would rather fly a passage falcon at partridge than at pheasant because of the aesthetic qualities of the flight itself. Partridge can be hawked without the aid of pointing dogs and these would be replaced with binoculars. The partridge would be espied sitting out, a falcon allowed to take to the wing and whilst she reaches her pitch, causing the partridge to clamp down and stay put, the falconer manoeuvres himself into position. He will then flush the partridge at the right moment, or at least attempt to. The partridge may well do their best to sneak off or indeed run rather than flush in front of the falconer. Personally, I far prefer to use a pointing dog; their work is a very great part of the beauty of falconry for me. With a dog pointing the covey, it is far more reluctant to move and the falcon will very soon associate the dog with the springing of game and will therefore give it her full attention. The flight at partridge is surely one of the most fetching in falconry, particularly when it is the Grey or English partridge that is the quarry.

As well as making ideal partridge hawks, passage tiercels can also be flown at snipe. This is a flight that is stunning, both in its setting and execution. Having seen first hand snipe hawking in Ireland I have to question now whether there is anything to match it for tiercels and grouse hawking for falcons. Perhaps, the only thing to come close would be hawking Sandgrouse in Morocco, which I was fortunate enough to do almost forty years ago. On that particular trip the falcons used were in fact passage Barbary Falcons.

IN THE FIELD

When it comes to taking to the field with the passage falcon then strictly speaking there will be two different mind sets offering themselves to the falconer and which one he will choose to take, will depend on what he is setting out to accomplish. The first will be concerning the passager that has come into his possession in the hopes of being rehabilitated at some point in the not too distant future and the second is for the falconer who is fortunate enough to have a legal passage falcon to fly and is hoping the partnership will turn out to be a long and very rewarding one. The mind sets will vary accordingly, because the former is very much a case, if at all possible, of getting the falcon up and flying again and proving to one and all that she is capable of surviving under her own steam. Accordingly, the finesse normally associated with training and flying passage falcons will not necessarily be applied. Making relatively quick progress in order not to mar the chances of a successful rehabilitation will be far more the order of the day. Whilst that certainly doesn't mean that things will be done in a slip shod manner the emphasis will be more on getting the falcon flying and killing, than having superb manners. By contrast the falconer lucky enough to have a legal passage falcon will take extra care over every single element of the training of the falcon and this will follow through into the way in which things are approached when taking to the field with the passager.

For the passager being rehabilitated, then the options for quarry are normally very straight forward. It will be something that is abundant locally, legal and that the falcon itself wants to chase. By that I mean some passage falcons will have already established in their minds certain species they like to fly and certain species they will only do so if taken down considerably in weight as an encouragement. Obviously the former is preferable as the intention is to release a strong, fit and healthy falcon. Some will fly corvids with gusto, some will really prefer not to, unless nothing else is available to them. In my circumstances, relating to land and all year round availability of quarry, then corvids are the ideal quarry for me to try and get a passage falcon onto. Being realistic then, a few kills are all that is required to assess if the falcon is fit enough to be released. Providing she shows no sign of being over tired or having an obvious debilitating repercussion, such as a drooping wing, then on kill number five or six she can have her limited equipment cut off whilst she feeds up on her kill and the falconer can retire to watch her finish her meal in safety. Then in all probability, the falcon will fly off a short distance, perch, preen and eventually take off. From that moment on she is on her own again and the falconer can only wish her well and be thankful that he or she had a small part to play in her survival and hopefully her onwards progress.

Should the passager being rehabilitated be a tiercel, then the choice is not so straight forward as the ideal quarries, starlings and magpies may not be so readily available. In any case starlings will require a quarry licence which may or may not be granted, depending on time of year and circumstances applicable to the particular area the tiercel is being flown in. Where I have helped with rehabilitating passage falcons and tiercels in central and South America then there really is no problem with quarry species. Boat Tailed grackles, Spur winged plovers, and ducks for six months of the year, are in abundance. No quarry species licences are required and probably the biggest hindrance of rehabilitating any raptor in such countries is the presence of large numbers of resident raptors, ranging from peregrines through to Red tailed hawks, White tailed hawks as well as Coopers and Harris hawks.

When my own career in falconry began, most falcons that came the way of the falconer were passage falcons of whatever species and because of the greed of the majority of trappers also a fairly high ratio of haggards. Although far from ethical for the falconer to be training and flying haggards dealing with the problem of trappers supplying them was a rather difficult one with no easy

Phillip Glasier, Walt Disney and James Robertson Justice

solution. An order would be placed with a trapper or dealer in a country such as Pakistan, India, Nigeria, Morocco or wherever and the order would specifically state no falcons in adult plumage. The falconer ordering the falcons would be notified that his order was ready to send and again it would be checked that the consignment did not contain any adult falcons, only passagers. Assurances would be received that all was exactly as ordered and shipping would then be carried out. Often as not on arrival what was forthcoming, would bear very little resemblance to what had actually been ordered. Once the falcons were here however, there was realistically no practical way of returning them and accordingly they would be flown. It must be remembered that at the time although there were considerably less falconers trying to obtain falcons than there are nowadays there was no domestic production of raptors to cater for the market. Falcons were never simple and straight forward to get now matter how we may like to look back and tend to see the good old days through rose coloured glasses.

Often as not the falconer would have one or two alternatives on his or her wish list and would have to compromise as to the falcon that was eventually settled on. An example of this is when I was employed as a professional falconer many years ago and the quarry my employer wanted to hawk was partridge. I set about trying to obtain two passage tiercels. None being available to me at the time I actually ended up flying passage sakrets for the first season and adding a passage tiercel to the team in the second season. The sakrets in question came from Syria and were beautiful examples, feather perfect and with clean and scab free feet. The latter was so often not the case with wild trapped falcons that had been caught by means of nooses. The sakrets did their job admirably and with a degree of style but they were not the falcon that was number one on the list for the flight.

Other falconers were faced with similar dilemmas and as often as not passage peregrines, be they tiercels or falcons, were never easy to obtain and to end up with feather perfect examples in good condition was exceedingly difficult. Bearing in mind how even Gilbert Blaine in 1936 moaned that passage falcons were almost a thing of the past and despaired at finding a regular and reliable supply. With this difficulty in obtaining exactly what was wanted, many falconers flew Saker falcons at rooks and pheasants, Lanner and Lugger falcons at partridge and it has to be said Gyrs of any description, in Britain in the late sixties and early seventies, could probably have been counted on both hands with fingers to spare. Import licensing was eventually brought into Britain in the early seventies and very gradually tightened up the loopholes and did eventually almost stem the flow of haggard falcons being imported along with passage falcons. It was not just the larger falcons that were being trapped and shipped regardless of their age and importance to the breeding populations. Small raptors such as Red Headed Merlins and Shikra hawks were also trapped and shipped regardless of age. I genuinely don't think that any falconer who saw the condition that some of these shipments arrived in, both in terms of the condition of the hawks themselves and as to how they were actually packed to be shipped, could ever think that the introduction of import licensing could be considered a bad thing.

Often on collecting a consignment from Heathrow Airport, opening the box and discovering what had actually been sent as opposed to what had been ordered was very interesting to say the least. Examples of this being I once ordered six passage Red Naped Shaheen falcons for myself and a group of friends. Despite repeated instructions and confirmation from the dealer that the shipment consisted of six passage females and certainly no haggards or males what we received differed somewhat from that. We actually received eight falcons. Two were indeed passage Red Naped falcons, one haggard Red Nape falcon, one passage male Red Nape, one passage peregrine falcon, a haggard and a passage Saker falcon. Finally one haggard Red Headed Merlin which was apparently added in case any of the falcons got their hoods off during the journey and were hungry !!.

On one occasion I ordered six Lugger falcons for myself and friends and on opening the box discovered four Luggers and two Red Napes. As the price paid was £4 per falcon plus shipping I didn't complain too heartily at this incorrect filling of the order. For once, things had very decidedly worked out in my favour. Even Lanner falcons that were brought in from Nigeria, Ethiopia or Morocco tended to vary from what was ordered. To the dealer wanting to fill an order and get money, whether the falcons concerned were haggards or passage, male or female seemed to make absolutely no difference what so ever. It was purely a numbers exercise, or at least that is how it appeared to be. Once the correct number of falcons ordered had been secured off they went to the person ordering them knowing full well there wasn't really much that could be done by the recipient to correct things. Finding a trapper or dealer that could be completely trusted was never a simple matter and accordingly names and addresses of such were guarded very carefully. For many it was more a case of relying on a falconer living in the country you wanted a falcon from to help you out and through kindness and the camaraderie of fellow falconers many passage falcons were obtained in this way. This was certainly true in my case and on occasion even making the required trip to obtain a passager legally and bring it back myself seemed the best of all options available.

What always needs to be kept in the forefront of the falconers' mind and I know I have mentioned it elsewhere in this book and do not apologise for repeating it, the hold the falconer has on any passager is at best a tenuous one. It takes very little for something to break that bond and a lost falcon will almost inevitably be the result. I am not saying that flying a passage falcon is like constantly walking on egg shells but the finer points of falcon husbandry and interaction must never be allowed to slip. Always be mindful to be careful and considerate in your interactions with the passager, particularly in the field on a kill or even on the lure. The extra effort will pay dividends in the fact that your relationship with the passager lasts several seasons as opposed to several weeks or months.

I have friends in other parts of the world, particularly Mexico and South America that do not put telemetry transmitters on passage falcons in their first season. They think that the risk of losing the falcon is so high why add an expensive transmitter to the loss as well. Personally I don't go along with this but that is how they do things and it is their country and quite simply their choice. One thing they also do that I have learned to take notice of, is to not fly a passage falcon when a north east wind is blowing. This certainly causes restlessness in the passager and changes her personality and outlook almost immediately. A calm well mannered falcon quickly becomes restless and inattentive and may well be lost if flown.

High winds are of no real hindrance to the passage falcon and in fact once back to her true fitness she will revel in them and show the falconer her true prowess and capability. It should be borne in mind however that flying at check in such conditions will be even more appealing and allow her to have a slight advantage over any intended quarry. Accordingly choose slips in such conditions with care. Even if flying at check ends in failure it is a very negative lesson learnt and to be avoided, if possible, at all costs. As can be seen from my thoughts expressed here in this book flying a passage falcon, in my humble opinion, takes a greater degree of care and attention to detail than would be the case with an eyass. However do not let me give the impression that it is all hard work, checking and double checking everything to the degree where the actual flying part in the field becomes something of a trial as opposed to what it should be, that is the pinnacle of pure falconry to be rightfully savoured and enjoyed. My personal view is that nothing easy ever gives the same degree of satisfaction as something achieved that has been brought about by hard work and diligence. The added bonus is that of course this added attention to detail and fine tuning of the falconer's own attitude and application towards handling falcons will enhance the relationship between himself and any future falcon regardless of whether it is an eyas or passage.

TAILPIECE

For me, writing this book has been something I have wanted to do for a very long time, in that training and flying passage falcons has always been the pinnacle of falconry for me. I am somewhat concerned that generations of falconers, certainly in the UK will probably never get the opportunity to enjoy what falconers of my era took almost for granted in our early careers. Other than perhaps a falcon coming the way of the falconer to be rehabilitated, the chances of training and subsequently hunting a passager seem very remote I am afraid. Some other countries, such as the United States, now have a limited take scheme whilst other countries still allow the taking of passage falcons for falconry. If I was a young falconer now and wanted to fly passage falcons, then I would not have much hesitation in moving to somewhere where I could fulfil my falconry dreams. There is no truer saying than "You are only here once and this is not a rehearsal". Mexico and South Africa still offer the falconer the legal opportunity to fly passage falcons and with the added pleasure of being able to trap the falcons themselves. So much better than in the 1960's when most passage falcons coming into the UK did so via dealers and usually arrived somewhat mentally scarred and certainly in need of a good imping session.

I am fully aware that each generation of falconers tends to think that falconry, as a sport, was better in their heyday than in that or those that come after them. In many respects this is true. When I first started to fly falcons there was no telemetry and certainly no domestic production of hawks. As the sport became more popular, you had more and more people chasing fewer and fewer suitable hawks and falcons. You only had to look through the pages of "Exchange and Mart" and "Cage and Aviary" birds and see what was being offered to know obtaining a decent falcon was exceedingly difficult. Lanners, Luggers and Sakers, along with Red Headed Merlins were probably the easiest to obtain but these would be offered alongside White Eyed Buzzards and Brahminy Kites. The two publications mentioned were the only place to look for hawks and falcons that were for sale, as there was no internet in those days.

No internet meant that communication between falconers was a great deal more limited and accordingly so was getting realistic advice quickly if the tyro falconer ran into a problem. Veterinary knowledge in relation to raptors, was also in its infancy. I am certain a great many falcons died from ailments that nowadays we would treat without any great feeling of concern as to the eventual outcome for the falcon. No telemetry meant that as often as not, a hawk misplaced chasing quarry very often turned into a lost hawk altogether. Added to this was the fact that the hawks concerned had been taken from the wild initially and accordingly reverted to their wild, instinctive selves very quickly indeed. If a lost hawk wasn't recovered pretty quickly, then even if sighted or found a few days later its recovery really was a very unlikely scenario.

Hawk food is another area that was nowhere near as refined for the falconer as it is now. There were no companies specialising in frozen hawk food and most hatcheries, certainly in my area, would not sell waste product day old cockerels because they went en masse for other purposes. Hours were spent each week with an air rifle ensuring a decent supply of quality food was available for your hawks. As can be seen from the above, the falconer's life today is certainly a great deal easier than it was thirty or forty years ago, at least that is the case in the UK, however there are many things that have degenerated as well as improved. When I first flew falcons almost fifty years ago it was estimated that there were around four to five hundred falconers in all of the UK and this included Austringers, who were in the majority, as well as longwingers and a handful of eagle enthusiasts. Now we have well in excess of twenty thousand people with hawks of one description of another. Obviously in amongst this number will be a great many that do not actively fly their hawks and probably those with owls also get lumped into this figure. Even so, if you said that

The author in Mexico with intermewed passage anatum Tiercel

merely one tenth of this number were active you have a great many more people seeking land to hunt on and also to exercise their hawks over. The increase in general leisure time and with most people nowadays having more disposable income than fifty years ago shooting has also increased greatly in popularity. This means there are now a whole host of people with sporting intentions badgering farmers and land owners for permission to have access to their ground. Add to this the need for our very small island to expand housing areas; the situation is getting quite dire. More and more people chasing less and less suitable ground which itself has less quarry than ever on it.

Also with our new age, comes new attitudes and not all of those are as we would like. I have lost hunting ground because others decided that it was easier to effectively poach on the ground I had permission on rather than bother to try and find ground of their own. I know of other falconers who have encountered the same problem. Another piece of conduct that will get all falconers tarred with the same brush and will also eventually, I firmly believe, have serious legal repercussions, is the habit of driving round areas in which the people with the hawks (I cannot bring myself to call them falconers) do not have permission and on, seeing something they consider suitable launch the hawk or falcon out of the window of a car.

One final thing I see as a very big negative and I am fairly confident I am more or less alone in thinking this, is that domestic production of hawks with emphasis on hybridisation has unbalanced things in favour of the falconer in relation to his quarry. For the flight of a peregrine falcon at rook or grouse is one where predator and prey are evenly matched and both have had their natural skills honed over the centuries so that neither one has a perceptible advantage over the other. The flight is a contest between two birds that in the wild have evolved simultaneously in a manner that allows one to predate upon the other with a success to failure ratio that is balanced by both species and thereby means both species have a tendency to have sustainable and relatively stable populations. Then along comes man with ever bigger and more powerful hybrids and accordingly there can be a shift in the balance of power so that it very much favours the falcon. I can personally recollect inviting a falconer to come and share a moor with me for a week as his own was short of grouse and showing no sport at all. He duly arrived with a simply massive Gyr cross Saker hybrid falcon and every time it flew, the biggest problem we had was getting the grouse to actually rise and take to the wing. They would far rather run and take their chances with the dogs than take to the air. The result was very poor sport because a sledge hammer was being used to crack a nut. The balance had shifted too far for things to be comfortable and the sport suffered accordingly. At the time of writing this book, a pure domestically produced peregrine falcon is approximately the same price as a grey jerkin and somewhat harder to actually get hold of. For years now peregrines have been used to produce large hybrids and accordingly pure ones are getting difficult to find. Just about every hybrid falcon combination you care to think of is being produced and so there is a serious risk that even fewer people will get the opportunity to seriously fly domestically produced peregrines at quarry, never mind passage ones.

With all these various factors being taken into account I decided it was indeed time to write this book, even if only for my own satisfaction of sharing some of the pleasure I have enjoyed and ensuring that the knowledge of training such a specialised hunting companion is passed on. I am not arrogant enough to say my way is the only way or the best way, only that it is the way that has served me well and helped me to enjoy some excellent sport over the years and enabled me to work in harmony with passage falcons, the pearls of falconry. I hope this book has been enjoyable and provoked some thoughts regarding training, if so then writing it has been a worthwhile expenditure of time.